MORE
AWKWARD
SITUATIONS
FOR MEN

Danny Wallace

MORE

AWKWARD
SITUATIONS
FOR MEN

EBURY
PRESS

1 3 5 7 9 10 8 6 4 2

First published in 2011 by Ebury Press, an imprint of Ebury Publishing
A Random House Group company

The Random House Group Limited Reg. No. 954009

Addresses for companies within the Random House Group can be found
at www.randomhouse.co.uk

A CIP catalogue record for this book is available from the British Library

The Random House Group Limited supports the Forest Stewardship
Council® (FSC®), the leading international forest certification organisation.
All our titles that are printed on Greenpeace approved FSC® certified
paper carry the FSC® logo. Our paper procurement policy can be
found at www.randomhouse.co.uk/environment.

Designed and set by seagulls.net

Printed in the UK by CPI Mackays, Chatham, ME5 8TD

ISBN 9780091941307

To buy books by your favourite authors and register for offers visit
www.randomhouse.co.uk

For Tiffany Daniel

Is there anything in this world cuter than burping a baby?

Yes.

Burping a kitten.

But oh no, 'society' frowns on that.

Gorbachev

Introduction

Hello there.

This is *More Awkward Situations for Men*, and my name's Danny Wallace.

You might remember me from that time on that train when I was daydreaming but it looked like I was just staring straight at your chest or phone or small child and you wondered whether you might need to alert the authorities.

Anyway, I welcome you to this book – a book packed with stories from my life at a time when everything had changed. When life was no longer just about me, or my wife, or my friends…but about a brand-new little man too, and all that that entails.

I think many of the events in this book – the awkward situations, the well-meaning faux pas, the inadvertent insults or slights which are given or received – apply to lots of us, whether male or female. The universal rules of polite society seem never to have been written down properly, and perhaps this is an attempt to remedy that just a little.

This is not a book you should feel you should have to read in one sitting, by the way. Please don't feel pressured. In fact, it's probably best if you read it in short bursts. If you identify with a particular story or event, maybe put the book down for a little while, so you can think long and hard about what that means and why you insist on living your life this way.

My thanks must go to the people of *ShortList* magazine – in particular Phil Hilton and Terri White – for allowing me to collect many of the pieces I've written for them and include them in this book.

I have done my best to tell these stories in the way I would tell them were we sitting down in a pub together, and I hope you like them.

Your round, by the way.

Danny Wallace
London, 2011

First of all...

First Things First

'Well,' I say, trying to make it sound like an important word, an *historic* word. But I don't quite nail the gravitas I was after, so I try it again three times. 'Well well well.'

We are standing by the ducks in a local park, and it is the day before my wife is due to give birth.

'Well well well well *well*.'

'Well well what?' she says, staring out over the pond, half-smiling.

'Well…this is probably the last time we'll ever do this. Just you and me. Walking through the park. A couple.'

My wife considers it, and doubles her half smile to a full one.

'I s'pose it is.'

And we walk home, holding hands.

That night, we're sitting in a darkened Turkish restaurant on the high street as a slanting rain batters the window. I've just ordered some small sausages and a beer.

'Well,' I say. 'Well well.'

'Well what?' she says.

'I'm just thinking. This is probably the last time you and I will do this. Just the two of us. The two of us – a couple – sitting down and having a romantic meal together.'

My beer and small sausages arrive.

'It's not *that* romantic,' says my wife, looking at them.

'No, it's not *that* romantic, no,' I say, picking up a tiny sausage, and pointing it at her, so she can see I'm serious. 'But this is probably the last time we're going to enjoy a not-*that*-romantic meal together. Because, as you know, we're going to have a baby, you see.'

'Yeah. I think *I* told *you* that.'

'I'm just saying. This is it. The end of an era. The end of coupledom. The beginning of...well...what would you call it?'

'Parenthood,' says my wife. 'You'd call it parenthood.'

'Exactly!' I say. 'That's *exactly* the phrase!'

And I eat my sausages and we walk home, holding hands.

Later, as I climb into bed, I hand my wife her healthy peppermint tea and I clamber over her bump.

'Just think,' I say, picking up my book. 'When we turn off the light in a minute or two, that'll be the last time we'll ever turn off the light as a couple, and then go to sleep as one, because tomorrow, everything changes. Everything. So we should just enjoy this moment, just as we enjoyed that last meal, and that last walk, and that last trip away, and that last drive-through McDonald's, and that last peppermint tea in your hand.'

My wife looks at me. And then she leans over and she gives me a hug.

'You shouldn't be scared,' she says, gently. 'It's going to be good. It's going to be *great*.'

I nod and turn the light off.

It's dark.

But the light comes sooner than expected.

By six in the morning, we're at the hospital.

And by 6.09 in the evening...we have a child.

And as I stand there, and as I pick him up, and as I hold him for the first time, and I look into his eyes for the first time, and I hold his hand and I kiss him for the first time, I realise that this is a *day* of firsts, and not a day of lasts, because out of nowhere I now know that life – the very *best* of life – is all about the firsts. Because it's the firsts that matter. The firsts are worth looking forward to; the firsts are worth looking back on.

That night, my wife sleeps quietly as our baby dozes on my chest, the streetlights blushing orange through the hospital window.

I place my hand on his back, and smile.

Then, a couple of days later, when the time is right and proper, my wife and I, we step out of our car – a little, fragile family – and we carry our son through the front door.

For the very first time.

And so we begin

The Lift

The lift is taking a while to arrive, but I am confident it will get here eventually.

I have taken all the necessary steps: I pressed the button; the little red light came on. Now my main function is to wait.

The display over the doors tells me that the lift is still on the sixth floor of this department store. It's been there a while. I give the button another little press for luck and step back and stare out across the shop.

Seconds later, a small harassed woman has arrived and stands next to me, tutting and looking at her watch. She tuts some more and it becomes clear she wants to involve me in her tutting, but I have no time to encourage other people's tutting today. She seems determined, though, and tuts and sighs and says, 'Oh, why is this taking *forever*?'

I smile and look at her but she quickly looks away, as if she has thought about it and actually she's too busy and too late to involve me in her tutting after all.

The lift's on the fifth floor now, but seems to have stopped again. Maybe it needs a little rest. I start to consider the stairs, but then – for the briefest flicker of a moment – the small, harassed woman *almost* steps forward. It was just a flinch, just a tiny movement, virtually imperceptible…but I'm onto her.

'I know what she's doing,' I think to myself, inwardly frowning, taking it in. 'She wants to press the button!'

She sighs again, and I can sense her rolling the thought around in her head some more.

'*Just press it,*' she's thinking. '*Only you can press it properly…*'

'She doesn't have the nerve,' I think to myself. 'She knows I have already pressed the button. The little red light is on. I've got this. Pressing the button *herself* would be a bold statement. She would be saying, "I do not trust this man to have pressed a button correctly. He must have pressed it wrong, even though there is only that button to press and all you can do with a button is press it. But I can press buttons *correctly*. If I press the button, I will do it slightly differently, and the lift will magically get here quicker than it will under *this* idiot's rule."'

I smile to myself at the thought, about how ludicrous I'm being, and as I do that her little fingers jab forwards and she presses the button again.

'No!' I think. 'You lunatic! I'd already pressed it twice!'

I steal a sideways glance at my new nemesis, this woman who thinks so little of me that she has to push my buttons for me, this woman and her curious and direct challenge on my abilities as a human male.

'Chimps can press buttons!' I fume to myself. 'They can teach squirrels and pigeons to do it! But oh no, this lady assumes I've made it through thirty-four years of life without ever happening to come across a button before. She probably thinks I've been here all morning, staring blank-eyed at the display, my tongue out, wondering when the magic metal box will arrive to change my surroundings!

'Please,' I start to think. 'Please don't let the lift arrive now by chance. If it does, she will have won, and worse, I may very well have to deal with the fact that I can't press buttons properly.'

But no. The lift makes no such appearance. The display tells us it's now on the third floor, and I'm filled with warmth and love for it.

'Rest, sweet lift,' I think. 'Take your time.'

The woman has started tutting again, but I am serene and calm. I would happily wait here all day, because *she* has pressed the button now. She was the doubter who wanted to take charge, and I have been proven right. Nothing would make me happier than to wait here for nine, ten hours, because it's not my responsibility any more. *She* is now to blame for the lift's non-arrival.

Maybe I should tut *her*.

And then a man arrives. He's busy and important and talks loudly on his phone. He jabs the button. Seconds later the lift door opens. He looks at us, as if to say, 'Why didn't you just press the *button*, you bloody simpletons?'

'What floor?' says the man, as we traipse inside, belittled.

'Six please,' I say.

'Two,' says the woman.

We know this is no longer our dominion.

So we ignore each other, and let him press the buttons.

The Doll

On a cold and frosty Tuesday morning, when our baby was still a couple of weeks away, we received an email from an eccentric aunt.

'I had the best idea,' it said, 'to help you with parenthood! I've just ordered it on-line! It'll be with you in the next few days!'

This was exciting. Exciting and mysterious. What could it be, this magical idea to prepare us for parenthood?

'Maybe she's got us a nanny,' my wife had said, puzzled. 'Or a baby.'

We thought about it for a moment, and then got on with other things.

Three days later, a package had arrived.

'A package has arrived!' I shouted upstairs, because packages deserve to be shouted about. 'It's for us!'

'Is that why it arrived here, at our house?' replied my wife, but I ignored this, because I was already ripping it open.

'Oh,' I said, finally. 'Hmm.'

'What is it?' said my wife, walking down the stairs.

'It's...a life-size rubber toddler,' I said, staring at it.

The doll stared back. But there was something else about this doll, and I was not sure whether I should point it out.

'So...I wonder why she chose a *black* toddler,' I finally say, and then I went all quiet, because I wasn't sure if what I just said was racist. 'I mean, I *welcome* this black toddler. Let it not be said that I don't welcome this black toddler. It just seems...unusual in its specificity.'

'Yes,' said my wife, slowly, also unsure of where the lines are when discussing the racial background of a small rubber doll. 'But we must embrace him into our family. We will call him...Didier.'

We sat Didier on the sofa, and within hours, it was like he'd been there all our lives. He fast became a useful tool. He reminded us constantly that soon, there would be a new, small person in this house. One we must *prepare* for.

Soon, though, we got a little too comfortable with Didier. My friend Wag came round, and we sit on the sofa drinking wine, and it wasn't long before Didier had a glass too, and my wife took a photo.

'Oh, that's a *great* shot of Didier,' she said. 'We'll have to use that for something.'

I struggled to see what we could possibly use it for, but I nodded along happily, because I didn't want to insult little Didier.

A week or so later, there was a knock at the door. I knew exactly who it was. It was the man I'd found on the internet who'd agreed to fix our computer.

'Come in!' I said.

The man was tall and black with elegant gloves and I asked him to sit down while I popped the kettle on.

'So,' I said, wandering into the living room. 'It's a Mac.'

'What operating system?' he replied.

'I'd have to check,' I said, handing him his coffee and sitting down opposite. And then I noticed something. Something *appalling*.

The man was sitting next to Didier.

'And what's the trouble?' he said.

My mind went blank. I had no idea. Because all I knew was, I had to get this man off this sofa. But maybe he hadn't noticed! Maybe he hadn't noticed he's sitting next to a small rubber black boy!

'Let'sgoupstairsandI'llshowyou,' I garbled.

My mind was racing as we traipsed upstairs. God, how did this make me look? I looked like Madonna, but on a budget. I was a Lidl Madonna!

'This is the computer,' I said, pointing at the computer, which seemed unnecessary, given this computer expert had probably seen a computer before.

He sat down and began tapping away. I was flushed with embarrassment and felt weirdly guilty.

'I could explain,' I thought. 'That way he wouldn't think it was weird. He doesn't know I'm married. Maybe he thinks I'm a single man who lives with small dolls.'

Instead, I spotted a copy of a PS3 game still in its cellophane wrapper, and then inexplicably said: 'Do you have a PS3? Would you like this game?'

'So we could set up a network here,' he said, after refusing. 'Have you got a laptop?'

This was my chance!

'My *wife* has!' I said. See? Not weird!

I bounded off to fetch it as proof.

'You'll be able to file share,' he said, turning it on. 'Plus share your music, your photos…'

'That'd be *great*,' I replied, and we both stared at the screen as it came to life.

And we *kept* staring.

Because as it turned out, my wife *did* use that photo of Didier.

As her desktop picture.

I cleared my throat as we took in the image. Me, enjoying a glass of wine, with a small rubber black boy.

'So, do you have an Xbox?' I said.

The Visitor

It is a breathtakingly peaceful Sunday and I am sitting in the kitchen reading the papers and drinking some tea when the doorbell rings.

I look at my wife. She looks at me. There is a silence.

I check my watch. It's two o'clock. Two o'clock on a Sunday.

The bell rings again.

I put down my paper and shrug at my wife, who looks terrified. Who could this be?

It can't be the baby – he's upstairs, asleep.

So who could this be, on a Sunday at two o'clock?

It is our friend Anna.

'I'm so sorry I'm late,' she says at the door, hugging me. I am confused. My wife must have invited her without telling me. I pretend I know all about it.

'No worries!' I say, grinning broadly. 'Come in!'

We walk into the kitchen.

'Anna's here!' I say.

'Hello!' says Anna, scanning the kitchen and seeing we've not really cleaned up or washed the dishes. And then she looks at me. I'm wearing pyjama bottoms and a *Ghostbusters* T-shirt.

'Let's go through to the lounge!' I say, confidently, as if I *always* dress this way to welcome guests into our home.

Moments later, I'm back in the kitchen.

'You didn't tell me Anna was coming,' I say.

'You didn't tell *me* Anna was coming!' she says.

'I didn't know Anna was coming!' I say.

'*I* didn't know Anna was coming!' she says.

'What are we going to do?' I say, desperately, and then a look of abject terror flashes across her face.

'New Year's drinks!' she says. 'She thinks she's here for New Year's drinks! Remember we floated the idea?'

I think back. Yes. Yes, we had. *Ages* ago. We'd even suggested the first Sunday of the year. But no one had mentioned it again. No one had *confirmed*.

'You know what she's like! She's going to expect champagne!' I say. 'We're going to have to find champagne!'

'There's a bottle in the fridge. That posh one your dad didn't want.'

I am thrilled. We can do this. We can pull this off. My wife leaps upstairs to put some proper clothes on, while I grab the bottle of quality champagne and some glasses and take it to the lounge.

'Happy New Year!' I say, showing off the label like we'd bought it specially, and then popping it. Anna looks delighted. Anna is someone who drinks a *lot* of champagne.

'So, am I actually *early*?' she says, pointing at my pyjama bottoms.

'No! You're bang on time. This is the time we agreed, isn't it? For the – you know – for the New Year's drinks we'd planned and are now doing?'

'Yes,' she says. 'So who else is coming?'

'Um…' – oh, God – '…I think it's just you.'

She looks a little uncomfortable.

'And Colin,' I say, quickly. 'My friend Colin.'

She relaxes a little. I excuse myself and immediately phone Colin, who is hungover and grumpy but agrees to come round. My wife bounds into the living room looking great and I leave to change out of my T-shirt and pyjamas.

When I get downstairs again, they are laughing and Anna has made good headway on the champagne. We are getting away with this. She is convinced we have arranged a wonderful event in her honour, complete with plenty of vintage fizz.

The doorbell rings. It's a dishevelled Colin.

'All right?' he says. 'What've you got to drink?'

'Champagne!' I say. 'The finest vintage champagne!'

He comes in and we pour a glass each and everyone is having a lovely time. And then I see the bottle is empty. I pick it up and ask my wife to join me in the kitchen.

'I think I can knock up some canapés,' she whispers. 'We've got some Philadelphia and that carrot.'

'We've run out of champagne!' I say. 'We've only got this stuff left!'

I hold up a bottle of supermarket own-brand sparkling white wine.

'I can't bring this out!' I say. 'She's going to think we're downgrading her!'

We both look at the empty bottle of proper champagne. And then I do something unforgivable. I pop the bottle of own-brand wine open and, while I hear a delighted whoop from Anna in the other room at her favourite sound, I take this cheap stuff and, with impressive skill, manage to pour it into the posh bottle.

'She won't know,' I say. 'It's all the same!'

I am brilliant.

I stride proudly into the living room with the now-full bottle.

'*Another* one?' says Anna, mock-shocked. 'You're *really* spoiling me!'

I make a humble face and then, the perfect host, begin to pour.

There is an awkward silence.

Anna stares at the glass.

'Why's that champagne bright orange?' says Colin.

'Happy New Year!' I shout, far too loudly.

The Bench

On my walk home from the station, I decide to stop off at the park for a few minutes to eat my sandwich. I choose a bench – one with armrests – and I sit in some unexpected end-of-winter sunshine, the only person on any of these benches, in this sweet North London park.

It's peaceful here, and I ponder quietly to myself as I notice an older man shuffling past the other benches, a newspaper under his arm and a blue plastic bag in his hand. I instantly like him, for no other reason than he is here, in this park, with me. We are two men of different generations but the same mindset, brought together by nature and chance. I imagine when he passes, we will raise our eyebrows at one another, as if to say, 'Peace, stranger. Fare thee well. Fate that our paths should cross this day,' and then something like, 'Live long and prosper,' but not that.

How nice it is, I think, that two complete strangers can be bonded by just a moment. That we will share something, for no more than a second in time, and how good it is that as humans we—

OhGodhe'ssittingdownnexttome.

I stare straight ahead. This is not the done thing. I subtly look around. There are *loads* of benches in this park. Some *terrific* ones. And yet this man's chosen to sit down on this one. Next to me.

I've not been munching my sandwich for a bit from the shock of it so quietly begin to eat again.

'He wants to chat,' I think, shaking my head imperceptibly. 'That's the only explanation. He sat down next to me in search of a *chat*!'

There should be no reason why him sitting next to me should be in any way uncomfortable. The bench is big enough for two. I am not averse to talking to strangers and indeed consider it something we should all do. It's just that when it's made so abundantly clear that a stranger wants to talk, the pressure that brings with it is huge. The more desperate they seem, the less inclined I am to want to join in.

The problem is, you can't just get up and leave. That's hugely insulting, and it makes you look as if you're the type of person who doesn't want strangers sitting next to them on benches, which we all definitely are, but which we all definitely feel is very important no one ever knows about us.

I realise I am trapped for a minimum of five to ten minutes.

'He'll probably just get his newspaper out in a second,' I think. 'I just have to play the waiting game.'

I close my eyes and pretend I am thoughtful and sunbathing. But it's like there's a ticking clock. We both know he has to make his move soon.

And then he coughs.

'This is it,' I think. 'This is how it begins. A noise to break the silence. A cough he can now excuse himself for or remark on or that will act as a lead in to something I won't know how to respond to, like, "Well, I wasn't expecting to see the *sun* today!"'

But no. There is no follow-up. He must have lost his nerve. But why? He was doing so well! He had the guts to sit down next to a stranger, he held off on opening the newspaper, *and* he coughed! This is sad.

It must be me, I think. I have been too closed off to his advances. Sitting here, staring straight ahead, or pretending I'm sunbathing. Who the hell do I think I am? Someone special? Someone who must not be disturbed? Someone too good to speak to a stranger who's taken the trouble to sit down next to me on a bench?

No! That is not me!

I must make this man feel better. But how?

I clear my throat.

'Aaah,' I say, like I'm enjoying how peaceful and perfect it is sitting next to this man on a bench. 'Well, I wasn't expecting to see the sun today!'

I look at the man. Nothing. He says nothing. And then he just nods his head slightly and says, 'Yup.'

Instantly, I know what he's thinking. He's thinking, 'Oh God, he wants to *chat*!'

But I don't! I don't want to chat!

He's also thinking, 'Now I can't move for five or ten minutes otherwise I look rude.'

So he gets his paper out, and I play Angry Birds on my phone, both of us properly fed up of the park.

Mr Barker

There's a knock at the door and I know exactly who it is. It's the man I've asked to come round and give us a quote for some shelves.

'Hello,' says the man, standing in a thin rain.

'Come in,' I say, opening the door wide. 'I'm Danny!'

'I'm Mr Barker,' he says. 'So – shelves?'

'Yes,' I say. 'This hallway, and—'

But hang on…

'I'm Mr Barker?'

'Yep, okay,' he says, and he gets out a measuring tape, but I'm no longer paying attention, because all I can think about is how he's engineered a situation in which he's called Mr Barker, and I'm just called Danny.

'Both sides of the hall?' he says, and I nod blankly.

Surely *I* should be the mister in this situation? I'm the man paying for this! Either we should *both* be misters, or *neither* of us should!

This must be some kind of clever trick, I think, suddenly paranoid. Like men in offices who make sure they're sitting on a slightly higher chair than you. Mr Barker has infantilised me. Mr Barker has made it so I can only ever refer to him as Mr Barker. If he does my shelves, I'll have to say things like, 'Would you like a cup of tea, Mr Barker?' or 'Would you prefer custard creams or peppermint Viscounts, Mr Barker?' and then Mr Barker – just because he's called Mr Barker – will say that none of that is acceptable and he'll send me out to the shops for coffee and Penguins.

'He's about my age!' I think. 'How come he gets to be a mister?'

Just then, my wife comes down the stairs.

'Hello!' she says.

I know what to do.

'This…' I say, and then I pretend I have momentarily forgotten Mr Barker's name. I pause and say, 'um', and make a pained expression. Mr Barker doesn't seem to mind.

'Mr Barker,' says Mr Barker, and my wife says 'Hello… Mr Barker.'

That's twice now Mr Barker has introduced himself this way! He's playing mind games! Surely the polite thing to do in someone else's house meeting someone else's wife is to drop the formality, or at least ape the level of formality set by the person whose house it is? I kick myself for going in too low. Why didn't I wait until my wife had already been in the room, and then say, 'I am Mr Daniel Wallace, and this is my wife, Mrs Daniel Wallace'? Because I am an idiot, that's why. From now on, I decide, my wife will be known as Mrs Daniel Wallace.

'Would you like a cup of tea, Mr Barker?' asks my wife, and I am annoyed. She's fallen right into his trap. He's *definitely* going to ask her to pop out and buy some Penguins.

'Great,' says Mr Barker. 'Now, was there another room you wanted done too, Danny?'

'Yes, *Mr Barker*,' I hiss. 'Follow me, please.'

Half an hour later, Mr Barker leaves without further incident.

'I am sick of these psychological games!' I say, and my wife looks at me, surprised.

'What?' she says.

'The crazy world of Mr Barker!' I say, but she still looks blank.

'How come he gets to be a mister, but I'm just called Danny?' I say. 'I'll tell you why. Because one day, when there's a problem with the work, he knows there's no way I'll be able to complain, because I'll have to call him Mr Barker, and psychologically he's already winning. It's like men with hats. You have to do what men with hats say. They *earned* those hats. Those hats make them slightly taller than you. Those hats imply authority!'

My wife picks up a magazine and starts to read.

'Well, I'll tell you what,' I say, pointing my finger. 'I'm not employing Mr Barker. *I* should be the mister, not *him*! And also, I'm going to buy a hat.'

'Call him and cancel all shelving and tell him about your hat plans,' says my wife. 'There's his card.'

She points at the coffee table. There's a leaflet for his company with a small business card stapled to the top. I am fiery and full of fury!

'I will!' I say, picking it up, and looking Mrs Daniel Wallace very seriously in the eye.

I call him and let him know we'd like to go ahead with the shelving, whenever's good for him, really.

Twins

It was a five o'clock start this morning and I stumbled out of the house in darkness, leaving a note for my wife to say I would meet her in the park at about eleven. The plan is to wheel our glorious new baby son around, stopping to look at trees and bushes, and then maybe have a sandwich on the grass and call it a picnic.

A *family* event! Though one with bleary eyes and sleep-deprived minds.

It's now five to eleven, and I scan the park trying to spot them, a couple of sausage rolls from Greggs in my bag.

And there they are!

I jog over, happy, but as I get closer I notice something disturbing.

I slow to an embarrassed walk.

'Oh, no!' I say to my wife.

'What?' she says, oblivious.

'Oh, *no*…' I say, again, more quietly this time.

I look at my wife. I look at myself.

We are dressed exactly the same.

How did this happen? It is a deflating and worrying moment.

I look her up and down, and point at her.

'How come you've dressed exactly the same as me?' I say, despairing, glancing round the park to see if anyone else has noticed.

'What are you talking about?' she says.

'Look!' I say.

Black-and-white Converse. Black jeans. Grey V-neck under a plaid shirt.

'I didn't know what you were wearing today!' she says. 'And anyway, my shirt is red while yours just has red elements.'

I shake my head and ignore her mad protest.

'We look like we're wearing uniforms!' I say. 'We look like we're in some kind of smug parenting cult! What will people say when they see us?'

My wife looks around the park. No one seems all that bothered. A man walks his dog. Two kids kick a can. But I am deeply embarrassed. Nobody likes a couple that dresses the same. Granted: this happened by chance and our uniforms do not exactly stand out, but this is *exactly* the same as when David and Victoria Beckham turned up at that premiere all dressed up in leather. It's creepy and uncool and there should be laws in place that prevent it.

'If someone we know sees us, I'm going to have to explain,' I huff. 'I'm going to have to say, "My wife and I do not dress the same, despite the visual evidence that makes a very strong case to the contrary."'

'I think it's sweet!' says my wife, delighted, and I look at her like we've just walked into a zoo and she's tried to throttle a sea lion.

'Couples should not dress the same!' I say, firmly. 'We're not living in the future! Maybe in the future they do that, but not now, not in 2010 in a park in North London! It's creepy. People will snigger when we walk past. How will that affect our son, having people snigger as we walk past?'

I point at our son, who idly bats a stuffed toy hanging from his pram, perhaps simply trying to make the best of things, trying to ignore his parents' disturbing ways.

The real problem is, my wife and I now look like we're making a statement. Like we're striding into the world, shouting, 'This is how we do things! Deal with it! We're *those* people!'

It is not British. What will she make us do next? Wear little hats? A cape?

I decide I will have to remove my shirt and make do with my T-shirt. I take out our matching sausage rolls and our matching drinks and we sit on the grass and begin to eat.

My wife thinks I've stopped talking about how we've dressed the same but I haven't.

'It's the shoes that make it look like this is a decision we've made,' I mutter, shaking my head, and something seems to snap.

'I'm going to dress like you *every* day,' she says. 'I'm going to make people think I'm your little brother.'

Has she gone mad?

'And then I'm going to dress our son in exactly the same way too so that we look like three strange Russian dolls. And then we're going to get glasses and follow you around as you go to meetings or whatever, and say things like, "People sniggering will affect our son!" and look around parks, scared.'

I stare at her and shake my head again, but this time pityingly.

She is being very stupid today.

Oh, hang on, I get it.

'So you're copying my *personality* now?' I say, and she nods, and eats her sausage roll.

The Burp

My wife looks horrified as she rushes into the living room, carrying our baby.

'What is it?' I ask, looking from one to the other, panicked. With a small baby in the house, panic is never more than a moment away. A strange rash, an unusual smell…stocks in Google have gone up 600 per cent since we started searching for any and all of them.

'Quick!' I say. 'What's the matter?'

'I…I was on the phone…' she says.

Oh, God. She dropped our son, didn't she? You always hear about people dropping babies! My wife must've dropped our son!

'And I was talking to that handyman, Mr Barker…'

Or maybe she dropped him *twice*! Maybe she dropped him, picked him up, and dropped him again!

'And I was trying to settle up for the shelving…'

No way. Is it possible she dropped him *three* times? What kind of monster drops a child *three times*? My wife, that's who!

'And I was getting the credit card out of the drawer…'

Don't say four times! Surely not *four*!

'And he was in my arms, sort of dozy and droopy…'

Out with it!

'And he hadn't made a sound, even though the call had been going on for, like, five minutes…'

I break out in a sweat. I look at the boy. He seems fine. Oh, great – he must be in shock. We are dreadful, terrible people.

'And then Mr Barker was saying, "Okay, then, thanks a lot", and I said, "Okay, Mr Barker, bye then!" …'

And then what? And *then what*?

'And then…just before I managed to hang up…'

I nod her on, wild-eyed.

'The baby did a massive burp.'

Oh.

'Well,' I say, confused but relieved. 'Sometimes babies burp. I thought you knew that. It doesn't sound like anything to worry about, and anyway —'

'No,' she says, shaking her head, and distressed. 'No, you don't understand! You don't understand *at all*! Mr Barker had *absolutely no idea* the baby was there! I didn't mention it. Why would I? He was sleepy and quiet, and all Mr Barker would've heard was me talking about shelving, and then saying good-bye, and then, right before hanging up, doing a massive burp!'

Ah.

'But that's not fair!' I say. 'That wasn't you doing a massive burp! That was our massive burping baby!'

'I know! But now Mr Barker thinks I'm the kind of girl who burps massively!'

This is dreadful. I try to calm her but she won't stop.

'He must think I'm the kind of girl who finishes *all* her conversations with a burp!'

'I'm sure he doesn't!' I reassure her. 'I'm sure he thinks you just finished *that* one with a burp.'

My wife puts our baby in his little chair and puts her hands on her hips, shaking her head.

'You'll have to call him back,' I say. 'Explain. Say it was the baby.'

'I tried. He didn't pick up. Why would he? Why would he take a call from a lady who just burps at him?'

'Or *I* could burp!' I say. 'You could call him again, and when he picks up, I'll walk around the room, burping! And you can be like, "Hey, what's with all the burping?" and show him it's not behaviour you condone!'

My wife sits down, sadly.

'I feel like I should have an ASBO,' she says.

I hatch a plan. Later, I phone Mr Barker.

'Hello, Danny,' he says.

It still grates on me that he calls me Danny, while I am forced to call him Mr Barker.

'Hello, Mr Barker,' I say. 'I'm just checking to call to see whether we've settled up or not. I haven't managed to speak to my wife about it.'

'Yes!' he says, cheerfully. 'All taken care of, thanks.'

There is a pause. This is where I intend to say goodbye and then burp. I want my wife to feel better! I want her to laugh! She watches me from the sofa behind her fingers.

'Well...bye then, Danny,' he says.

'Yes...goodbye, Mr Barker...' I say, and this is it, this is my chance, this is when I should burp, to save the day and trick him into thinking it was in fact *me* who burped earlier and not my wife or son!

But I can't do it. I *like* Mr Barker! And the line clicks off.

My wife raises her eyebrows at me, our baby in her arms.

'It must be terrible to be as rude as those two,' I think, wisely.

The Pizza

My wife is out visiting friends with our baby, but before she leaves she tells me that I have to make sure I eat properly.

'I *will*,' I say, making a childish face. But secretly, she doesn't know how well I will eat. Because Colin is coming round for lunch and he's told me not to worry.

'I'll take care of it!' he'd said. 'What do you fancy? A delicious pizza, perhaps?'

'Oh!' I'd replied, delighted. 'I *love* delicious pizzas!'

'I do *too*!' he'd said, amazed at the coincidence. 'They're dee-*licious*!'

I am quite excited all morning. I try and get some work done but I keep glancing at the clock at the top of the screen in case it's already magically lunchtime. Every now and again I peer out of the window, because you never know, Colin might be early, and I could very easily see him walking up the steps to my door with that delicious pizza.

I can't help but wonder what flavour he'll choose. Perhaps he'll choose a Mighty Meaty. That's if he goes to Domino's, of course. If he goes to Papa John's, he'll probably get the Il Carnivoro, which is just like the Mighty Meaty, except with different meat.

'But…' I think, as I make another cup of tea to stave off the hunger pangs, '…he might walk past Quality Pizza. Or PizzaFace. In which case he'll probably get a meaty one.'

And then the doorbell rings.

'Here we go!' I think. 'It's pizza time!'

But I am disappointed when I open the door.

'Where's the delicious pizza?' I say.

He's wet from the rain and he's carrying a limp plastic bag.

'Aha!' he says, striding in. 'I went one better!'

What? You can't *get* 'one better' than a delicious pizza. Maybe he means he's got *two* delicious pizzas in that small limp bag.

'I went to the *deli*!' he says, proudly. 'It's my new thing!'

This is strange. Colin does not go to delis. He thinks olives are just chewy grapes. He whips a small blue box out of the bag and holds it up.

'It's a make-your-own-pizza kit! We're going to make our *own* delicious pizza!'

His eyes are shining from the emotion of it all.

'How do you *make* pizza?' I say, taking the box.

'There are instructions,' he says, and I see that he's right. But there's a problem.

'These instructions are all in Italian,' I say.

'I realised that. I was very angry. But then I remembered. You can *translate* stuff nowadays. You just type it into Google!'

Ten minutes later and we have a printout. I stand with a mixing bowl and the flour, ready to make the base. Colin reads to me.

'You spread the paste on the sheet of paper from furnace in the confection,' he says. 'So as to be covered all the surface.'

I nod, and try and do as he says.

'You poured over the polpa of tomato that it inside finds of the kit, a bit of rooms.'

I nod again, but don't really know what to do.

'It put into an oven and you make to cook approximately for ten tiny.'

I'm just staring at him now.

'I'm not really sure our cooker *does* ten tiny.'

'Then, add the other ingredienti to devout waxes. Servants quickly.'

His face falls.

'Hang on. What other ingredienti do we *have*?'

I fling open the fridge. There is a slice of ham, some processed cheese and an orange pepper. Colin looks sad, but he is determined to make his idea work.

'Well…we'll have an orange pepper pizza!' he says, with grim determination. 'It'll be dee-*licious*!'

I am not sure anyone has ever made an orange pepper pizza before, and when we are finished, we spend quite a lot of time staring at it. If a pizza could look like the seventies, it would look like this.*

The disappointment in the air is palpable.

'I guess we'd better cook it,' I say, quietly. 'For ten tiny.'

Ten tinies later and the pizza looks a little smaller than we'd imagined, and a lot more orange. We've essentially cooked a little orange pizza.

'This will be delicious!' says Colin, unconvincingly.

'Yes!' I say, joining in. 'Our little orange pizza is a triumph.'

My wife comes home and stares at the last slice.

We order a Meat Feast, and Colin says he's not going to go to the deli any more.

---

* *fig 1, appendix*

The Mother

I am walking through town when up ahead I see a lady I've met only once, through a friend. We do that thing where neither person knows whether the other is going to stop, and we sort of half-slow down and smile broadly but keep moving as we judge what the other's interest in stopping is.

But then I realise she's not going to stop, so I smile and say 'hi' and keep on going.

And then she stops and I look rude.

To make up for this, I spin round and begin to behave in an unusually friendly manner.

'Great to see you again!' I say, loudly.

'And great to see *you*!' she says, at the same volume.

We've now established a level of volume and friendliness that neither of us seems all that comfortable with.

'What have you been up to?' I say, again a bit too loudly.

'Oh, *LIFE*!' she says.

'Ha ha!' I say, and I nod a nod of understanding, and start to back away. 'Well…'

'Just so busy with the kids,' she says, moving closer, and so I quietly say, 'Oh dear.'

'Yes,' she says, nodding mournfully. 'Jess is thirteen now. You know what thirteen-year-olds are like.'

I laugh and nod again, even though really, I don't.

'Anyway…' I say.

'Have you *met* Jess?' she says, looking as if she's trying to rack her brains for any evidence of my having met her thirteen-year-old daughter.

'I've only met *you* once,' I say, and she makes a big face which seems to mean, 'Have I got a treat for you!'

'Oh, she's great!' she says. 'A real little lady now. I've got a picture here…'

She fishes in her bag for her phone and turns it on. I sigh, inwardly. It's cold, and we're outdoors, and I don't really need to see a photo of this woman's thirteen-year-old girl.

'God, I can never work these things…' she says, fiddling away, and I smile indulgently. I start to drift off while she taps at her phone.

'Swing by HMV,' I think. *'Grab a Nando's. Or maybe a burger.'*

'Gosh, I'm so sorry,' she says, all of a flutter. 'I'll find it in a second…'

'Need a new printer cartridge. Light bulb. Maybe two if I'm in the mood.'

'Aha!' she says, suddenly. *'Here* it is!'

She finds the right photo and thrusts the phone outwards. She looks deeply proud and I get ready to say the right thing.

But then I look at it. And I don't quite know what to say.

'She's such a lovely girl,' she says, willing my response.

But I am immediately uncomfortable. Because this picture isn't really what I was expecting.

'She looks very…confident.' I say.

'She made that outfit herself!' says the lady.

'Did she!' I say, trying not to look like I'm not looking. 'It is a confident look.'

'And she loves her make-up.'

'She certainly seems to have embraced it,' I say. 'So anyway…'

'That's just an old T-shirt I used to have in the eighties,' she says, pointing it out. 'And what she's done is just cut those holes there.'

'Yes,' I say, still not looking at it, but rather at other people walking by. I hope they are not looking at this woman's phone.

Because if they are all they will see is an inappropriate picture of a child.

'Well, there you are,' I suddenly think. 'I'm a man in my thirties standing on a street corner while a woman shows me inappropriate pictures of a child.'

'She'll be fourteen next week,' says the lady, shaking her head in disbelief, and I wonder if that makes it any better. Why couldn't she have shown me this next week? That'd probably take *days* off the prison sentence! And why can't this woman see that her daughter thinks she's in her twenties?

'She'll be getting a boyfriend soon, I imagine,' says the lady. 'Though I'm not sure she's ready.'

I smile.

'She looks ready to *me*,' I say, and then I realise that this sounds *bad*.

I freeze.

The lady looks again at the photo, and then at me, and she quickly puts her phone back into her bag.

'Well, I'll see you again someti—'

'Yes,' she says, 'bye!'

I am still shaking my head as I walk into HMV.

I pick up a DVD and join the queue. I realise I'm surrounded by lots of young girls from a nearby school. I lose my nerve and quietly go home.

The Drive

We're in the car on the way back from Sainsbury's when I pause at a corner to let another driver in. I smile magnanimously and double-flash my lights and make a cheery face. I'm enjoying the moment and how gracious I am being with my power.

My wife sighs.

'What's up?' I say, turning to her.

'Nothing,' she says, pretending to fiddle with the radio.

'It's because I'm polite, isn't it?' I say, turning back to see a Micra darting in behind the first car.

'It's because you're *too* polite.'

'I am *not* too polite,' I say, testily. Behind me, a van honks impatiently, but there's nothing I can do about it because now a Volvo's darted in, too. 'And anyway, there is *no such thing* as too polite.'

I make an imperious face and start to move forward, but I have to jam on the brakes again, because now some rude boys in a blinged-up Cosworth have barged their way in.

I smile and nod as if they've thanked me and slowly increase my speed.

On the way home, I start to wonder whether my wife thinks I am less of a man for allowing strangers to join slow-moving traffic. I am hurt as I think about it. Who would she rather I was? Some angry-faced lout with no sleeves who bullies and cajoles? A road-rager?

I quietly seethe.

Oh, yeah. Road-ragers. That's what she likes. She probably watches *Police! Stop! Action!* and really fancies all the blokes in it – the ones on the wrong side of the thin blue line. *That's* who she wants me to be. Someone with a flagrant disregard for not only the basic laws of the road, but also – and perhaps especially – a flagrant disregard for the feelings of my fellow motorists! She wants Jeremy Clarkson, that's who! She wants big-faced Jeremy Clarkson and his leathery limbs, and she wants him to do skids and wheelies right outside the police station and then do a twos-up and drive away.

I shake my head. That's *exactly* what she's like.

Or that lottery winner! The ASBO one, who spent all his cash on rally karts he'd drive round and round the local bus station! *That's* who she'd be happy with!

Oh, I know my wife *very* well.

'And anyway,' I say, suddenly. 'You're an incredibly aggressive driver.'

'What?' she says, startled.

I realise that neither of us has spoken for the last ten minutes, and this might *seem* to have come rather out-of-the-blue.

'I'm just saying,' I say, quietening down. 'You're a very *aggressive* driver. Very…belligerent.'

'I'm a belligerent driver?' she says.

'Very much so, madam.'

I pull up outside our house and I do not mention this again.

Two weeks later, we are on our way to a friend's place, somewhere outside London. The traffic is heavy and bustling, and we're already late, but there's a car off to my left that seems to have been waiting to join our queue for *such* a long time. I slow down, and double-flash my lights.

My wife sighs.

I decide to say nothing. But I will show her. I will show her. The man in the car looked delighted, and perhaps that is reward enough, but I am going to demonstrate to her what it's like to be with the other kind of man, the ASBO Clarkson lottery winner man, so at the next junction, I do not let anyone in.

She doesn't seem to notice.

But then, on my right, someone indicates that they'd like to join my lane. Ha. Not likely. No way. Not today. For I am *Clarkson* and I have *rally karts*. I do not yield, so they attempt to *barge* their way in, but I speed up, and I sense my wife's growing excitement. We're in the middle of a face-off! The man's indicator is still going, and he's still trying to get in, and this time I nudge my wife and say 'Not on *my* watch, chum!' and then I scoot in front of him and then – very quickly in the rearview mirror – I *give the man the finger*.

My wife laughs, delighted, understanding my rather shocking joke.

And then, as I stop laughing, my thoughts return to the road ahead, and I am forced to slow down.

Right down.

My neck prickles as we join the traffic jam. We are to spend the next twenty-six minutes trying not to be anywhere near the man to whom I've just given a suddenly not-so-jokey finger.

'*Now* look what you've done,' I say, wishing I could hit reverse.

'You shouldn't have been so belligerent,' she says.

I feel we've both learnt a very valuable lesson.

Trust

The man in front of me at the cash machine is taking his sweet time, but I can only wait, because there doesn't seem to be another cash machine for miles.

He keeps sighing and pressing more buttons, and on the odd occasion that he turns around to see if I'm still there, I do that thing you do in cashpoint queues, where you pretend to be really busy and fascinated by everything around you, in case the person in front thinks you're secretly a member of Fagin's gang or you've got a periscope and a pencil and you're trying to nick their PIN.

Eventually, I hear some beep-beeps, but instead of taking any money out, the man turns to face me, and says, 'It's broken, mate.'

'Broken?' I say.

'Run out of money,' he shrugs, and then begins to walk off, down the street.

This is tricky, socially. This is the only cash machine I've seen round here. And yet this man has told me the cash machine is *empty*.

'I should trust him,' I think. 'Why would he lie?'

I begin to walk away. But then…

'Or…what if he just couldn't get any money out?' I think. 'What if he was just saving face? Perhaps he is a proud man. Perhaps he cares too much what others think of him!'

I stop walking, and see where he's gone. He's nipped into the fish and chip shop on the corner.

'I could creep back,' I think. 'Try my own card. Maybe he just did it wrong. Maybe he put his Caffè Nero card in by accident, or his driving licence. Perhaps he's just not very bright.'

But no. I cannot do this. Trust in others is important. If a friend had tried to get money out and said the machine was broken, I would believe him. So why not this man?

I am sometimes like this with directions.

'Excuse me,' I'll say. 'Do you know the way to Acton town hall?'

And the very second they point in a direction, I'll think – based on *no evidence whatsoever* – 'I'm pretty sure it's not that way', and have to wait for them to disappear before walking off and following my heart.

'He's still in the chip shop,' I think. 'So long as he remains there, I am safe. So long as he doesn't come out and catch me flagrantly disregarding his advice, all is well. He *cannot* know I do not trust him. He will be *heartbroken*.'

Quickly, I jog back to the cashpoint and insert my card.

'Quick!' I think. 'Quick!'

The machine has a little trouble taking my card at first, and it spits it out, and I have to wait for the Welcome screen to flash off, and then I offer it the card again, and *finally* it takes it. This is just like 24.

Behind me, I hear a lady unzipping her handbag and, nervous, I turn and smile. She does that thing you do where you pretend to be really busy and don't have a periscope.

I glance once more at the chip shop, then back at the screen, and it's asking me to enter my PIN, so I do, and then press Enter.

The machine starts to think about something.

'Come on!' I shout, internally. 'Work! Prove yourself!'

Again, I look at the chip shop, and the man is still nowhere to be seen. I'm going to get away with this! I hear a beep, and I hear my card being returned, and all I need now is to take my cash and run, but when I look, what I see is...

SERVICE CURRENTLY UNAVAILABLE.

He was right. The man was *right*.

I take my card and I turn and face the lady.

'It's broken,' I say.

'Broken?' she says.

'Run out of money,' I shrug.

I turn on my heel, and walk up the high street, trying to find another machine. As I pass the chip shop, I see the man, sitting by the window, staring out towards the rainy grey city with a sausage. I nod at him, and he nods back wearily, as if to wish me luck on my quest, and it reminds me of the lady behind me in the queue. She too must now be searching out an alternative.

I turn back. To my horror, I see that she now has her card out, and is trying the machine for herself.

'But I *told* her it wasn't working!' I think. 'I *told* her!'

She glances towards me. I shake my head, absolutely furious with this arrogant woman, and I think about what a shame it is that not everybody is as trusting as me.

The Goodbye

I have had a lovely night with an old friend and as we pay the cheque and stand up we both agree we have to do this again.

'Definitely!' I say.

'Definitely!' he says.

We put on our jackets and brace ourselves for the cold outside, and outside the restaurant we stop for one last second to shake hands and make sure we both absolutely understand that we really should do this again.

'Definitely!' I say.

'Definitely!' he says.

'Okay, well…'

And we go for the hug. We do it well. It's a success.

And then we both start to walk in the same direction.

'Oh!' I say. 'Ha ha! Are you going this way too?'

'Ha ha!' he says. 'That's awkward!'

'Ha ha!' I say again, to make it less awkward, although this just makes it a bit more awkward. 'Ha ha!'

There is a quiet moment as neither of us knows quite what to say.

'So…that was fun,' he says, and I nod, but I can't help but feel we've already had this conversation. 'We should do it again, like we said we would.'

'Yes!' I say, clapping my hands together. '*Definitely*.'

'Yes,' he says. 'That would be good.'

I look up ahead. So does he. Not far now. We're nearly at the main road, which presents us with a myriad of escape opportunities. If he starts to go right, the rules state I'll have to go left. I can always double-back in a few minutes, when the threat of the multiple goodbye has subsided.

We fall silent as we reach the road.

Then: 'So…'

'Yes,' I say. 'Well, safe home.'

'Absolutely. And I'll give you a bell about doing it again.'

'Definitely,' I nod.

But what now? Do we hug again? We've already hugged once. But then, we've said goodbye *twice*.

There is a moment of nothingness as we try and work out how it works.

I decide to go for it.

'Heeey,' I say, smiling, arms out, but he's gone for the hand-shake, and now I'm too close to pull out, so I squeeze him hard and feel the back of his limp hand on my chest as I crush it.

'Love to the missus,' I say, as I release him, and I start to make my way round him, so I can catch my bus, but then the worst thing possible happens.

He starts to go that way too.

It is slight, and it is subtle, and he's stopped himself, but we both know it's happened, and now there is no way out.

'Ha ha!' he says. 'You're going this way too!'

'*But I was first,*' I want to shout. '*The rules state you have to go the other way and then double-back if necessary!*'

'This is so funny,' I say. 'Ha ha.'

'Ha ha,' he says, but I can see he is already eyeing up the next corner and working out his strategy.

'So are you getting the bus, or…?' I say.

If he's getting the 214 to King's Cross then I'm going to have to get a cab. If he's getting a cab I'll get the bus. We cannot extend this to a shared journey. We have exhausted our conversational resources. We've already agreed to do it again, countless times, plus two goodbyes and 1.5 hugs.

'I might get the bus, yeah,' he says, which is strange, because he doesn't seem to know. 'Or maybe the underground, if there's one close.'

He has no idea where he is. So how does he know where he's going? And then it hits me. What if he's been attempting double-backs all along? What if he's been trying to see which way I go, and then I confuse him with an unwelcome hug or I move too quickly? We are going to have to be very, very careful with our next moves.

We cross the road and up ahead I see the bus stop.

'So,' I say. 'There's a bus. A bus that goes to King's Cross...'

'That's quite handy for me,' he says.

'Or there's a minicab office just over there.'

'Hmm,' he says. 'What are you doing?'

'I thought I might get the bus,' I say.

He looks at his watch.

'I should probably get a cab,' he says.

Phew. Good lad.

'Well, then,' I say, offering my hand. 'Let's make sure we —'

'Definitely,' he says, as we finally go our separate ways.

'Danny!' he says, the next time we meet.

'Hi! How are you?' I reply.

I am still standing at the bus stop. It's been five minutes. He's been told there are no cabs.

'Sooo,' I say, wondering if I'll need to hug him again.

The Pants

It's a bright and sunny day and so naturally I am deep underground on a stuffy and airless tube train, tired after another sleep-deprived, baby-based night, and on my way into town to undertake simple errands.

I have finished my newspaper and I'm glancing around the carriage when I put my hand on my leg and I notice something.

A lump.

'That's strange,' I think, frowning and subtly tapping at it.

But this is a soft and malleable lump. One that shifts about and gives.

And then I gulp.

Because I think there's a loose pair of pants in my trousers.

'Oh, God…' I think. 'I just pulled these jeans on at the last minute. I was wearing them yesterday. But they must still have had yesterday's pants in them.'

I bristle, and look around the carriage to see if anyone else has noticed.

'Please don't notice,' I think. 'Please don't notice there's a loose pair of pants in my trousers.'

This is not fair. I'm permanently exhausted. And a loose pair of pants is the last thing I need. A loose pair of pants is the last thing *anyone* needs. How do I deal with these traitorous idiots? Do I get them out? How? Do I just shake my leg until they're jolted free? I'd look like some new kind of mad pant-terrorist! Or do I do the sensible thing, and merely take a deep breath, stand up, slowly unbuckle my belt, and reach in?

I look at the lady opposite me.

She might not like it if I stand up, slowly unbuckle my belt and reach in.

The problem is, this pair of pants are like an undergarment time bomb. At some point, they *will* pop out. They will *definitely* pop out. But when? They could choose to pop out at any moment. It could be right here, right now, but if I don't do something, if I don't *take charge*, it could be *later*, when I'm walking up the stairs of the tube station, with a vicar behind me and a group of schoolgirls just in front.

My friend Laura once went through something similar.

She'd woken late one day in a panic and dashed across town to make an important business meeting. She made it with seconds to go, managed an impressive performance at the meeting, but upon walking to the door heard someone say, 'Oh my *God*!'

'What?' she'd said, spinning round, to see several people in suits crowded around a small pair of pants on the office floor.

'It's someone's pants!' said one of the men. 'Someone's left their pants here!'

It was then that Laura recognised them. Recognised them as *yesterday's pants*.

'Who would do such a thing?' said a lady, horrified.

'This is *awful*!' said another.

'What must you think of us?' said a third.

Laura just shrugged. 'What kind of business are you guys *running* here?' she tried, then turned on her heel and confidently headed for the door.

But I do not have the luxury of a door to turn on my heel and head for.

Plus, I think turning on my heel might cause the pants to pop out.

'Maybe if I tie my boots really tight I can tuck my trousers in and create some kind of dam system,' I think, and I immediately lean forward to put my excellent plan into action. But as I do so, I can feel I've loosened the gap by the knee, and something begins to slide slightly. I freeze. This moment is critical. If I move too quickly before the dam's in place, I'll initiate the pop-out.

This is *just* like *Mission Impossible*, or that bit in *Raiders of the Lost Ark* when all the booby traps go off.

The slide slows to a halt. But I must hurry. It's my stop next. I know if I stand, the slide's already in action and the pop-out will be next.

'I hope it's not pants,' I think, sweating. 'I hope it's some socks. I will consider the day *a total success* if it's just some socks.'

I leave the train and am immediately bustled into a crowd.

'Not now,' I think. 'Please not now.'

I hop onto the escalators and feel the slide about to start up again, like the moment in a film where a car teeters on a cliff.

'Please, no vicars,' I think. 'No vicars or schoolgirls!'

But then – away from the crowds and out of the station – my attitude changes completely. My pants are a burden and I must be free.

It occurs to me that I have reached a stage in life where nothing at all would make me happier than to allow a pair of pants or socks to slide out of the leg of my trousers and lie, twitching and obvious, on Europe's busiest shopping street, so I might stride away, my head held high, my triumph obvious and my trousers unburdened.

And I can't work out if that makes me the most mature man I know, or the most unsavoury. I decide to err on the side of caution.

I duck into McDonald's. I spend the rest of the day with a sock stuffed in my pocket. Sometimes I wonder if my friends realise how lucky they are to know me.

The Thing

There is a fox who has started to visit my garden. I have named him Didier, because we have a doll named Didier, and whenever I've had to name something lately, I have named it Didier, because I'm tired and it's just easier to name everything Didier.

Stalking into my garden late at night, or clattering over the corrugated iron of the garage next door, he stares up at me through my window with his big fox face. We stare at each other under the light of the moon, when I'm sitting at my computer not doing my tax return, and I find myself fascinated by him, like Tony Soprano and his ducks, and I wonder what it can mean that we have developed such a special connection.

He seems to have started to visit my garden more since my last birthday, like some kind of subtle message from mother nature. Perhaps he is saying, ome, look into my wise old fox eyes. Share in my wisdom. The wisdom of the fox. Adapt as I have, as the world around you changes. For you are a man now, my son; you are a parent, a father.'

But that is just the problem. I am so tired and sleep-deprived as a parent, a father, that I fail to pick up on his foxy wisdom. Instead I think the thoughts of a simpleton, like, 'Hey! There's that fox in my garden!' or 'What do foxes like to drink? I've only got Lilt. Do foxes like Lilt?'

And then I get back to not doing my tax return. *Everything* is better than doing my tax return. 'Oh, to be a fox,' I think, 'and not to have to worry about forms and tax and deadlines.'

But while I'm thinking this, Didier has another plan altogether…to challenge me as the alpha male in my own home.

One day, the night after one of Didier's visits, during which we'd stared mournfully into each other's eyes for a few moments before he'd vanished into the bushes, I spotted something odd in my garden. I went outside for a closer look, and there it was…*whatever* it was. It was grey, and it was slushy, and it seemed to have two stumps where legs might have been…and it was disgusting. Absolutely *disgusting*.

'Didier!' I cried out. 'What have you *done*?'

I poked at the Thing with a stick, thinking I could perhaps move this loose-skinned carcass into a bush or behind a tree and pretend I'd never seen it, but what was left of its bones gave way, and I dropped the stick and ran back inside.

'I'll make a cup of tea,' I thought, slamming the door and locking it, just in case this headless, legless mess was still alive and after revenge, 'and then I'll do my tax return or something.'

But inside, I slowly came to a realisation. That…*thing*… wasn't going anywhere. And this was *my* house. And I was the *man* of this house. And I *was* a man. I was a *grown-up* man. For the first time in my life, I felt absolutely and totally responsible for a task. There was no avoiding this. No delegating. This was my mission. Like my own tax return, I was the only person in the world who could do this. I *had* to do it.

I'll do it later, I thought, and finished my tea.

Later, I looked out of the window at the Thing.

'Why would Didier do this?' I thought, shaking my head. 'I thought we were friends. Is it some kind of challenge? A gift?'

I decided that I really didn't want to get into gift giving with a fox. They'd always come out of it better than you. Even if all you gave them is vouchers, somehow they'd get away with giving you bits of moss or dead things. It's the same with toddlers. When will they take responsibility for decent gift giving?

With a heavy sigh, I started to form a plan for the removal of Didier's grand statement. I would have to scoop it up with some kind of flat, metal tool and then put it...somewhere. I could bury it! In the garden! But I don't have a spade.

Hey – the bin! Of course! I could just put it in the bin! But then I'd have to walk it through the house, trying to avoid smearing it on any walls as I took it out the front, and how would I explain a mark like that to my wife when she got home? 'That? Oh, that's from a rat or a pigeon or something. See how it offsets the pure white walls!'

I shook my head. I was being outfoxed. But again...what had been Didier's thought process? Was he teaching me a lesson about responsibility? But I knew about responsibility! I was a father! A father with a tax return not to do! Or...was he indeed challenging my very manhood? Was he hoping that when my wife saw I was incapable of removing a dead who-knows-what from our garden, she'd kick me out and let the fox move in? Was I destined to stare mournfully up at my own window, while Didier sat at my computer, chasing the mouse and drinking my brandy?

No. No, I had to do this.

I went inside to find a dustpan and brush, just like Bruce Willis in an action movie. I would *show* Didier.

And then I played Xbox for a bit instead. And then I looked out the window. And then I shut the blinds, and I sat down at my desk, and with a heavy sigh, I did my tax return.

'This is a *bit* like being a man,' I thought. 'I am doing my tax return. That is something even Didier probably avoids doing. But I am facing this task head-on. I am a *man*. I am just not a *real* man.'

The Thing was gone the next day. Didier must've taken it.

He's not been back. I think he's disgusted with me.

Paranoia

Something very odd has started to happen to me.

Since I hit my thirties, I have not, as was planned, turned into a grown man. I have, instead, turned into a little old woman.

I'm sitting in a café with Colin. He has a small piece of sausage clinging to the side of his mouth and some egg down his top. And he's just seen me do something strange.

'You just saluted that magpie,' he says, with an accusatory tone to his voice.

'No, I didn't,' I say, startled. 'I was scratching my forehead.'

'You *did*,' he says. 'You just saluted that magpie! Why did you salute that magpie?'

'I didn't salute it!' I say. 'I just have a very itchy forehead. I've always had a very itchy forehead. You know that about me. That's why they call me…Captain Itchy.'

'Who calls you Captain Itchy? I've never heard anyone call you Captain Itchy. And I've been watching you. Whenever that magpie's flown by the window, you've saluted.'

He's right. I have been saluting the magpie. I have to. It's good luck. Who knows what could happen to Captain Itchy if he didn't salute the magpie?

'You realise that saluting a magpie has absolutely no effect on your life, don't you?' says Colin. 'You realise that it's not really Satan in disguise and that the events that do or do not occur in the world around us can in no way be down to magpies? There's not going to be an earthquake or a pile-up just because one man in a café in North London showed a bird disrespect…'

'…No,' I admit, begrudgingly. 'But I can't help it. The worst thing is, I have to do it with both hands. Once with my right hand, and again with my left, always in that order. And if someone's seen me do it I have to pretend I'm just scratching my forehead and do it all again. It can be very time-consuming.'

'So you're not just superstitious?' he says. 'You've got paranoid OCD as well?'

'It gives a sense of balance,' I say, desperately. 'I don't know whether you're supposed to do it with your left hand or your right hand and so I do both!'

'Oh dear,' says Colin, suddenly realising that that bit of sausage was still there and pushing it into his mouth. 'Well, that probably just negates the gesture. The magpies will know that. They probably find you annoying, toying with them like that.'

We both look out of the window. The magpie has settled near a bench, and is studying a Chicken McNugget. He doesn't look all that annoyed. Nor does he look like he has any concept whatsoever of humans, cafés, or what a salute is. But still it takes every inch of my self-control not to suddenly snap my hand to my head to try and ensure he won't rain down his evil upon me. If that's what magpies do. I mean, I'm no expert.

But a few years ago, for a TV show, I did attempt a short experiment on luck. For one day, I did everything that was deemed unlucky. I opened umbrellas indoors, I put new shoes on the table, I cracked a mirror and I spilled salt without throwing it over my shoulder straight afterwards. And on the second day, I wore green (which apparently the good-luck fairies really admire), I spent eight pounds buying eight scratch cards all called Lucky 8s, I carried a rabbit's foot about and I made a friend dress up as a chimney sweep and then cross my path. On both days I placed bets at the local Ladbrokes. On the first day

I lost my money. On the second day, I doubled it. And won twenty pounds on the scratch cards. And – best of all – received word of a small and unexpected tax rebate. I don't know if it was the rabbit's foot, the fairies or the Inland Revenue, but *something* was on my side that day.

'Nonsense,' says Colin. 'Luck is just probability taken personally. You were doing things, so things were going to happen to you. If you hadn't bought the scratch cards you wouldn't have won on them. Whether or not you'd put some new shoes on the table would have had no effect whatsoever. What – do you think there's some deity taking notes on your behaviour and checking to see whether all the mirrors in your house are in good working order before rearranging some scratch cards in a shop? Do you really think he'd have time for that? That'd take *ages*.'

'No…' I say, sheepishly. Colin has caught me out. Where has this behaviour come from? Why do I do it? I am no better than a medieval simpleton scared of the moon. I'd probably burn a witch given half the chance. Why can't I be more like Colin? Colin doesn't defer to magpies; Colin is a *proper* man.

And then I try something.

I reach over, grab his salt shaker, and pour some salt onto the table in front of him. It is a brave and unexpected move. I am fighting this!

Colin's eyes meet mine, in horror.

'You idiot!' he says, shaking his head.

And then, after a second or two, he sighs and tosses some of it over his shoulder.

I bravely resist.

On the way home, some way up ahead of me, I spot the television actress Su Pollard. She is carrying a large plastic bag with her, and some keys in her other hand, and as she tries to switch hands, she drops the bag and looks upset with herself.

I can't help but feel responsible. I have upset the delicate balance of the universe. But I must be brave. There will be victims of my behaviour, and Su Pollard is probably just the first. I must brace myself for any news I might hear about her. I salute, twice, and hope there's a magpie watching.

Interesting Man

I've only just met the man I'm with but already we're getting on like a house on fire.

I could stay here all day, just chatting to him. It's as if all the other guests at this party are mere extras in the scene where I meet the really interesting man in a film called *Meeting the Interesting Man*.

He's midway through a brilliant and interesting story about a book he's read where the main character moves to post-war Germany as a teenager. It strikes a chord with me. There's something I just have to tell him and it's now or never, because it won't be relevant the second he moves on.

'*I* used to live in Germany!' I say. 'When I was a kid. Just for a year. But that's funny that he did, too.'

I'll be honest: it seemed more interesting in my head.

'Oh, right,' says the man, raising his eyebrows. 'Anyway…'

And he continues to tell his story.

'This is great,' I think. 'It's bonding!'

And then – incredibly – he mentions that the man who wrote the book married an Australian.

Well, I have to tell him!

'Ha!' I say. 'That's just like me! She's from Melbourne, my one.'

'Oh! Melbourne,' says the man, smiling, and then he swiftly continues to tell his story, which, although it's getting better and better, he subtly seems to be losing the enthusiasm for. I don't want that to happen, because maybe that means we're not bonding in the way I'd thought, so I make sure he can see I am fully engaged in his story. I nod and smile and make shocked faces at the appropriate times. And then he mentions Mauritius.

'I actually know a guy from Mauritius!' I say. 'A hypnotist. He's got the world's only Hypnodog.'

The man looks a little crestfallen when I say this, but surely there is no reason to be. If anything, I've been showing just how interested I am in the story in the first place, by chipping in with a fascinating fact about a hypnotic dog. But his face seems to tell a different story from the one his mouth is telling. It seems to be saying, 'If you were truly engaged in my story, you would shut up and let me tell it. I have told this story on many different occasions in many different settings – to princes and paupers across continents vast – and it goes best if not part of a double-act. Although I am pleased you once lived abroad and know of an unusual dog, that is not really the point of this story.'

I am shocked and embarrassed by what I'm reading into, and quietly say, 'Sorry – go on…'

'Oh my God, I am boring,' I think, as he resets and continues his story, his eyes now darting around the room, perhaps nervously seeking out an escape. 'I am a boring man, being all boring. If we were at the credits sequence for *Meeting the Interesting Man*, you'd see my name next to "Boring Man at Party". I am like one of those people who says "fora" instead of "forums" or "stadia" instead of "stadiums", like they expect everyone around them to clap and be impressed at their conscious decision to be a dickhead.'

I am filled with embarrassed self-loathing. Because I'm being that person who manages somehow to relate everything the other person says back to themselves. And those people are *terrible* people.

I watch as the interesting man's mouth moves open and shut and know that if he is to soar, I must set him free. I must make a series of tiny sacrifices – in this case a sequence of related anecdotes – so that he can feel he has done his job as an entertaining party guest. *Then* I can tell him about marrying Australians or hypnotic dogs.

He mentions France.

'*I'm* going to France this summer!' I think, desperately. 'But I must not tell him that!'

This is killing me. But a story has its own special rules. No longer can it be considered a mere subsection of a conversation. You must respect The Story, for it is an intimate performance of great risk but mutual reward. And so somehow I remain silent and engaged and focused on looking like I'm actually listening to what he's saying.

And then he reaches the end.

'…and he eventually ended up retiring in Switzerland,' he says.

I check it's the end of the story by saying nothing for a moment. He looks to me for a reaction. But I have no idea what to say.

'Switzerland?' I think. That's the end of the story, is it? What am I supposed to do with that? This clown's been wasting my time. It was all build-up. If anything, my interruptions have *saved* this story. But now there's an anti-climax to deal with. A gap to fill. I have to ask him a relevant question about his story that shows I am interested and unselfish.

'My *mum*'s actually from Switzerland,' I blurt out.

'Oh,' says the man, clearly hoping that this next scene in *Meeting the Interesting Man* is a very short one indeed.

Simple As, End Of

Colin's upset because a girl he's been working with has said something highly offensive.

'It was unnecessary, Dan,' he says, as we walk to the Post Office. 'And it really cheesed me off, if I'm honest.'

'Talk me through it,' I say. 'Allow me to be your sounding board. Be specific.'

'She's just...*one of those people*,' he says. 'Y'know? One of those people who *says those things*.'

I think about it.

Nope. Nothing.

'You're going to have to be even *more* specific.'

Colin clicks his fingers.

'Like, yesterday, I was telling my story.'

'Ah yes. Your story. I like your story.'

'And I got to the bit where I do the accent.'

'The bit at the end? That's a good bit.'

'Yeah, and so I do the accent, and everyone's waiting for the punchline, and then she saunters by right behind me and says, "Oh! Was he Welsh, was he?" But as you know, Dan, he wasn't Welsh, he was Australian, but everyone laughed more at that than they did at the punchline. It didn't sound Welsh at all, I don't understand why she said that!'

'That's just a thing people do,' I say, waving his concerns away. 'If someone does an accent they purposely misplace the accent for comic effect, even when said accent is actually geographically very accurate. I wouldn't hold that against her. It's instinct with these people.'

'It's belittling.'

'Well, I'm belarging you back up again. Your accent work is just super.'

'Another thing,' he says, as we arrive at the Post Office.

'Why did you want to go to the Post Office again?' I interrupt.

'I didn't. I thought you did.'

We turn around and start walking the other way.

'Another thing,' he says. 'She says "literally" too much. She says things literally get up her nose, but I bet if you looked, they don't. The other day she said she walked past a dog and it woofed and she literally jumped out of her skin. She didn't. That would be *disgusting*.'

I make a face that says tell-me-about-it and then quickly make another one that says not to. I look up and see that that bloke who's always in Greggs is in Greggs again.

'And!' says Colin. 'She's always saying she's "obsessed" with things. Like, kitsch things that no human could ever really be obsessed with.'

'Please elaborate.'

'She'll say, "Oh, you guys, I've become, like, totally *obsessed* with Lemmy from Motörhead's hair." It's like a never-ending quest for the quirky. *No one*'s obsessed with Lemmy from Motörhead's hair. Have you seen it? It's like even *Lemmy*'s lost interest.'

He carries on, waving his arms about and ranting, but I stop listening and just wait for a pause.

'I hate it when people say, "Simple *as* – end *of*",' I offer, when it comes.

'Do you mean you hate it when people say, "Simple *as*", or are you including "End *of*"?'

'I am including "End of" in that, yes.'

'Right. I wasn't sure if you were just using it.'

'You think I like "End of" but I draw the line at "Simple as"? You must think me a very complex man. Anyway, I think you're being harsh on this girl.'

Colin stops and looks at me very seriously.

'She calls people "sweets". She says "totes" instead of "totally". The other day I was asking her where she likes to go of an evening, and she said "Londinium town".'

'She invoked Latin?'

'She invoked Latin. Plus, Dan, she'll tell you something horrible, and then she'll say, "I'm only being honest." Like that's some kind of laudable personality trait! Like it deserves credit! Like that makes rudeness okay! She must say it ninety times a day. "Sweets, you've got bad hair and you stink. I'm only being honest." No! This is honest: you're a horrible person. If everyone was like you, we'd be at war, all day, every day, and there'd be no such thing as diplomacy! It'd be Nazi Germany all over again, I'm telling you.'

And then something dawns on me.

'Why were you asking her what she likes to do in the evening?'

'Hmm?'

'Why were you asking her that?'

'Well…friendly banter?'

'Were you asking her out?'

'Yes.'

'What did she say?'

'She was *very* honest.'

'I see. Are you going to try again?'

'She said it literally broke her heart to say it. Called me "Sweets". That's a good sign, right?'

'Totes,' I say, nodding. 'End of.'

Conversation Starters for Ladies and Gentlemen: 1

TOPIC 1

I think deadlines would be even more effective if we called them deathlines.

TOPIC 2

My wife said to me recently that she hates couples that finish each other's sentences for them. I agreed that it was annoying, but it made me think that perhaps we were missing out on something, so now every time she says anything, I say 'full stop' at the end.

I have been doing it for a full week now, and it has really kept the romance alive.

TOPIC 3

It is strange how if you call someone a 'woman', the image it conjures up is less intriguing or seductive than if you call them a 'lady'.

However, the very opposite is true if you're talking about Catwoman or a Cat Lady.

TOPIC 4

Everything is different Down Under. We're up, they're down and, thanks to the Coriolis effect of the southern hemisphere, bathwater swirls the 'opposite' way down a plughole.

This must be hard to deal with. But did you know that they also have to play Swingball the opposite way, too?

This is the tragedy of Australian life you never hear about.

TOPIC 5

I think a good job to have would be measuring distances with a trundlewheel, because let's say you got stuck talking to someone really boring, you could just say 'excuse me, I just have to measure how far away you are' and then you could take your trundlewheel and walk off.

Not only would their feelings be spared, but you would learn a new fact, and facts are important.

And then...

The Stranger

'Ah ha ha!' I giggle to myself. 'Ah ha ha ha!'

I am in the local shopping centre and I am giggling to myself because I have seen my friend Paul milling about outside the cinema. He's with a couple of people I've not seen before and they're clearly considering which film to watch.

'Ah ha ha!' I giggle to myself again.

It has become a rather demonic giggle – not that you get many giggly demons – because I have mischief on my mind. Proper, childish mischief. It is the kind of giggle I'd make in the garden as a kid as I crept up on my sleeping dad with a bucket of water; the kind of giggle your face can't hide.

'Oh, this is going to be brilliant,' I think to myself, as I sidle through the crowd towards him. He's still not seen me, because now he's pointing up at the posters, and checking his watch, and saying something to the others that they seem to be agreeing with, because they're nodding, and checking their watches too, and then one of them catches my eye as I creep up behind Paul, and she scrunches her nose and tilts her head as I put my finger to my mouth and make big, elaborate steps, before *grabbing* Paul's midriff with two hands and then *tickling* him and shouting, *'Hello, cheeky!'*

His friends look delighted, but Paul shouts *'Jesus!'* and spins round, pushing me away, and then there's an awkward silence when I realise that, hang on – that's not Paul.

A couple of people who've heard me loudly bellow 'Hello, cheeky!' slow their walks and look toward us, smiling, clearly expecting to witness a better reaction. But there is none. I stare at the man for just another millisecond, trying somehow to *will* him to be Paul.

'Oh,' I say, slowly. 'God, I'm sorry. I thought you were my friend Paul.'

The man looks shaken but nods his understanding. His friends smile stiffly. I apologise again, and attempt to walk away with my dignity intact, and as I do so, I start to hope they are not talking about me and what has just happened, but on reflection this seems a little unlikely.

'Never tickle a stranger,' says Colin, later, in a café, as he spills tomato soup down his front.

'I didn't tickle a stranger.'

'You tickled a stranger. You walked right up to him, bold as brass, in a shopping centre, and you *tickled him* and called him cheeky.'

'But I thought he was Paul! The whole point was, I thought he was Paul!'

'That wouldn't have been Paul,' he says, shaking his head dismissively.

'How do you know? It looked *exactly like* Paul!'

'Just doesn't sound like something that would happen to Paul. Being tickled by a stranger.'

'But it *wasn't* Paul! It *didn't* happen to Paul! It happened to some other bloke!'

'That's what I'm saying. Not very Paul-like. Tripping over in the theatre, yes. Tickled by a stranger, no.'

I am confused by Colin's logic. We seem to be both agreeing and disagreeing at the same time.

'You can be a very embarrassing friend to have sometimes,' he says, leaning back in his chair. Most of the soup seems to be down his front. He can only have had about two mouthfuls.

'It wasn't my fault,' I say, and I'm about to continue, but Colin's face suddenly lights up.

'Hey, guess what I've got in my pocket?' he says.

'I have absolutely no idea.'

'A candy phallus!'

He beams, delighted, but who says *candy*? Who says *phallus*?

'Keep your voice down,' I say, scanning the room for witnesses. 'Where did you get it and why are you telling me?'

'No one minds talk of a candy phallus, Dan. It's the kind of saucy seaside postcard humour for which this country is famous.'

He gets the small candy phallus out of his pocket and places it on the table, and points at it and smiles.

'Ah ha ha!' he giggles.

'So, anything else, lads?' says the café owner, suddenly there.

I pick up the candy phallus and put it in my pocket.

'No, thanks.'

The man walks away.

'Great. Now he thinks I'm the kind of man who'd bring a candy phallus to a café and then pop it on display.'

We leave, but as we get outside, Colin seems troubled.

'What is it?' I say.

'Hmm,' he says.

'*What?*'

'Just doesn't seem a very "you" thing to happen, that's all,' he says, considering it. 'Paul, yes.'

He nods to himself.

'That would *definitely* happen to Paul.'

The Text

There has been an announcement on the 14.30 to Carlisle. We are running approximately four minutes late. Seeing as there's still three hours to go, I find it a little curious when the older lady on the seat opposite suddenly says, with wild and rising panic in her voice, 'I'd better tell Leanne.'

I'm sure it'll be fine, I want to say. It's only four minutes. And it's ages till we get to Carlisle. But then, I don't know Leanne. Maybe she's an idiot.

The lady rummages about in her bag and finds her phone, and begins to compose a text, which will presumably say: 'We are going to be four minutes late. Do not call the authorities.'

But it does not say that. It says, 'HELLO' so far, and I know that, because the lady is saying the words out loud and, with each keystroke, her phone is joining in with an incredibly loud BA-BLEEP.

And I mean incredibly loud. The kind of loud you'd reserve for attracting the attention of someone who is several miles away and has never had ears.

'WE' says the lady, slowly, with two more BA-BLEEPS.

I look around the carriage. People are looking up, and looking at *me*, as if *I* have something to do with this, as if I've somehow asked her to turn her phone up as loudly as she possibly can. I avoid their gaze, suddenly feeling very guilty. I concentrate hard, and read the first sentence of my newspaper: *A police spokesman said the man may have been…*

'ARE' says the woman, with *three* BA-BLEEPS this time.

I want to look at her now, to somehow let her know what she's doing and how annoying it is, but that would mean letting her know she's annoying people, and as much as I want her to feel *bad*...I don't want her to *feel* bad.

'RUNNING' she says, and because that's a much longer word, I now want her to feel bad.

So I look up at her, and make a small rustling sound with my newspaper, but it does nothing, so engrossed is she in making sure Leanne knows there is a chance she *might* have to wait less than five minutes.

She's onto the next BA-BLEEPS now. I try again with my paper...

A police spokesman said the...

Jesus. This word is taking forever. I try and guess what it might be.

'APPROXIMATELY' she says, and I kick myself, because of *course* it was approximately. I get back to my paper.

A police...

'FOUR' she says, and there are *four* BA-BLEEPS this time. So I make a little sniffing sound and rustle my paper again, pretending I'm reading intently and might well appreciate a little quiet, and yet she just doesn't notice.

'MINUTES' she says, and then, after the words 'police spokesman' have become burnt onto the back of my eyeballs, 'LATE'.

And I smile to myself. Because it sounded like there was a full stop when she said that. A subtle dip, an air of finality. My shoulders relax. There is a wonderful nothingness, a glorious silence. I give my paper a happy little shake, and continue to read.

A police spokesma —

'SO' says the woman, *very* loudly and with grim inevitability, the BA-BLEEPS now somehow more piercing and more jarring and more *evil* than ever.

'MEET' she says, and now I'm almost crying, because I just don't know how many more BA-BLEEPS a man can take, because what if she's about to make complex and lengthy plans, and what if Leanne needs everything spelled out for her in huge and unnecessary detail, and what if the next three hours are packed to the brim with BA-BLEEPS and words said out loud, and...

Then she stops.

And she chuckles to herself.

And she turns to her partner and says, 'Oh, what am I sending *this* for?'

And she smiles and rolls her eyes, and *then* she says, 'I'll *call* her!'

The Room

I have been summoned to the fancy café because Colin has big news.

'It's big news,' he says, sitting down, 'but it's *great* news.'

'Sounds like great big news!' I say, delighted. 'So what is it?'

'I…am growing up!' he says, and he toasts me with the giant McFlurry he bought on the way. 'I have a three-stage plan I'm about to set into motion. I realised recently – I need to move on. Progress. A man needs to develop his interests, widen his social circle, sharpen his mind.'

He studies the menu. His finger hovers for a moment over the sensible, egg-white omelette, but I know he'll end up going for the Full English, because Colin *always* ends up going for the Full English.

'So what's this three-stage plan?' I ask, curious. 'And what's stage one?'

'Stage one, Dan…is moving.'

I balk. 'As in moving *house*? To where? Why are you moving?'

He just looks at me, as if I've really not understood this whole growing up thing at all.

'I am moving because I spend all my time either in the pub or recovering from the pub. I need to move somewhere where temptation is not always on my doorstep. Somewhere I can develop my crafts, hone my skills.'

'You're not a samurai,' I say. 'What are these skills?'

He ignores this, and instead tells me the area of London he's moving to. I have to get my phone out and google it.

Famous residents, I find out, are Timothy Spall and the singer Gabrielle. It doesn't sound like the most *exciting* area he could've chosen.

'That's the point!' he says. 'Imagine the work I'll do! The money I'll save! Gary's got a spare room in his new place he says I can have for a while. I'll move there, and then it's on to stages two and three.'

'What are they?'

'I'm not sure what stage two is, but stage three is marriage.'

He snaps his menu shut and orders the egg-white omelette. I guess he is serious about this.

I am proud of Colin, I decide, as I traipse home. It is good for him to grow up, to make changes, to shake things up. And it is a good idea to develop a three-stage plan, even if stage two is a little hazy at this point.

I go home and tell my wife that Colin is moving away, that life is about to change, that no longer will we be at each other's beck and call, able to meet up, swap wisdom, set the world to rights. That Colin is growing up, and will now probably be attending adult learning seminars with his new friend Timothy Spall, or swapping pasta tips with Gabrielle. She looks at me, concerned, and makes me a cup of tea to cheer me up.

Colin moves away ten days later.

That night, I hear nothing from him. I go to bed, shaking my head, sadly.

But the next morning, there is a text waiting. He wants to meet me later, at the pub.

'Yeah, it's not working out,' he says, looking around the place, like it's been *years* since he's been in a pub, as opposed to forty-eight hours.

He gets his phone out and shows me a picture.

'This is my new room,' he says.

It is the smallest room I have ever seen. And it has very interesting wallpaper.

'That's interesting wallpaper,' I say, 'for a grown-up.'

The wallpaper has little teddy bears holding balloons on it.

'Colin,' I say, 'you appear to have moved into someone's nursery.'

'I know! It's a bloody *nursery*! At *no point* did Gary mention it was a *nursery*!'

'You can't live in a nursery!' I say, and then my eyes widen with the horror of what I'm about to say, 'What if you bring a *girl* back?'

'I know!' says Colin, his arms all over the place. 'I've had to develop a living-room strategy!'

'You've got too many strategies!' I say. 'What's your living-room strategy?'

'I'll have to keep them in the living room until the crucial moment, and then rush them into the teddy-bear room and hope they just don't notice.'

'That's a terrific strategy,' I say. 'But the next morning, Colin! The next morning they'll *wake up* and *look around* and realise *they're in a nursery*!'

He puts his head in his hands.

'This could really affect my chances of attaining stage three,' he says, gravely.

We both stare at each other for a moment.

'How's stage *two* coming along, by the way?' I say, standing to get us another pint.

'I think stage two will be moving back,' he says.

The Surprise

I read the email again and nod to myself. So far, so good. This surprise is really coming together!

'Dear Susan,' it reads, because this email is aimed at a Susan. 'I found your excellent website tonight and would like to arrange a surprise massage for my wife, whose birthday it is on Thursday.'

I giggle to myself. My wife will love this.

'She is very tired and achy from picking up and feeding our little baby and I thought it might be nice for her to start the day with something special.'

I pat myself on the back, mentally, for my efforts and consideration.

'Could you please let me know how much this will cost and whether you have anyone free at 9 a.m. for an early session. Many thanks.'

I press Send and sit back and wait.

An hour or so later, I have an email. It's from Susan!

'Hi, Danny. Yes, we have someone available at that time. Elena will be with you at 9 a.m. for a one-hour session with your wife. Please understand at the moment we only accept payment in cash, paid direct to your therapist.'

'That's odd,' I think. I read on.

'How about you?' it says. 'Can we tempt you to have one too? Might be nice! Susan.'

'Ha!' I write back. 'No, no. This is my *wife's* present. I'll just make them tea and observe!'

But then, as I press Send, I wonder whether Susan's idea *is* a nice one. I mean, maybe if the baby's asleep, I could probably get a very quick one in? After all, am I not stressed and sleep-deprived too? Am I not a modern man? Am I not *worth* it?

I click back onto Susan's company website and notice a picture of Elena, who looks quite glamorous. Next to her are pictures of lots of other young women in tight tops, smiling intensely. There is an FAQ section, and I click on it.

And that's when I see this sentence:

Money paid is for massage service only. Anything else that may happen between two consenting adults is not to be taken as inducement for payment or anything other than already stated.

Hmm.

'That's a strange thing to write,' I think to myself. 'They're a bit defensive, aren't they? It's a massage service! It's not as if they're prostitutes!'

Oh God.

They're prostitutes.

'What have I done?' I think, panicked. I think there is a chance I might just have inadvertently ordered my wife a prosti-tute for her birthday! The surprise element would be terrifically effective, and it would certainly be a story we could look back on, but I'm not sure the actual gift itself is entirely appropriate.

I fire off an email to Susan, with some urgency.

'Susan!' it says. 'I'm so sorry and please don't be as embar-rassed as I am. I'm going to have to cancel Elena because I think I just realised what your website actually is! Ha. And whoops. I'm very sorry!'

Send.

That was close, and I allow myself a moment of levity. I read through our exchange again. Of course: the cash payments; the young, glamorous women; the use of the word 'session'; the over-the-top disclaimer.

I start to think I probably shouldn't have said that I was just happy to watch.

Still – disaster averted!

But Susan replies straight away.

'WHAT?' she says.

Uh-oh.

'*Please tell me EXACTLY what part of our website gave you THAT idea.*'

Susan is angry. I have angered Susan! I type back, quickly.

'It's no big deal!' I start. 'I guess the bit about consenting adults and anything else that may happen. And the whole paying in cash thing.'

'*I can ASSURE you,*' she responds, within thirty seconds, '*this is a TOTALLY legal business.*'

Susan seems stressed out. She should maybe get a massage or something. But now, by trying to make things better, I have made them far worse.

'I am very sorry for implying you are a pimp, Susan,' I type. 'Or a madam. I now know you are neither a pimp *nor* a madam.'

Everything goes quiet. I sit there, hoping for a reply. I don't know whether Susan has cancelled the booking or not.

Eventually, her reply arrives.

'*Fine,*' says Susan. '*Elena will be there on Thursday at nine.*'

I wonder whether I should try and bond with Susan again by writing something light-hearted.

'And what about "extras?"' I write.

I think if Elena turns up it will be a lovely surprise for us *all*.

Queue-munity

Ꮖam minding my own business in the queue at Sainsbury's when I hear a loud pop and I jump slightly.

Someone has accidentally burst a balloon, and everyone does that thing that people do when they've heard a loud pop that turned out not to be gunfire. We all make big exaggerated faces at one another as if to say, 'I wasn't expecting to hear that pop just then!'

It is then that I notice something is not quite right.

The woman who had been behind me in the queue – who had arrived mere moments after me but who nevertheless *was* behind me – is now standing right *next* to me.

Well…sort of. She's still technically a few inches behind, but I can feel her presence by my side, as her bag sways into my elbow. She is far too close! And these are not the rules! She should be standing directly behind me, silent and bowed, respectful of my standing within the queue-community.

'Queue-munity,' I think, and I almost write it down, but then I realise that even if I start a Facebook group it will *never* catch on.

'Perhaps she was frightened by the sound of the balloon,' I reason. 'And sought shelter in my shadow. I imagine her senses will slowly return and she will rejoin the queue in her rightful position.'

But a minute or so passes, and as we shuffle forward towards the checkout and another blank-eyed shopper like us returns to society clutching their Nectar points to their chest like a gift from the gods, she remains right there, right beside me.

'What's she playing at?' I think. 'She must have been in queues before! Who are these people that think they can bring their own rules to the queue?'

Then it hits me.

'French! I bet she's French! I have had these troubles with the French before! They think someone's going to fire a starting pistol and then whoever gets to the till first wins! But we have a system in Britain! A system that does not account for starting pistols!'

Actually, maybe that's what she thought the balloon was.

But no. I am being culturally insensitive and wrong. And also, she is clearly not French, because now she's on her phone talking with an English accent about whether she should get a cab to the place for the thing tonight.

'You will get your cab, madam,' I want to hiss. 'But not at my expense!'

Soon, though, I start to weaken. I feel under a strange but enormous pressure to just avoid the hassle and allow her in front of me. But I cannot yield. If I yield, I am weak, and who is to say the person behind her will allow me to rejoin the queue?

But I know what she's up to. This is a slow overtake. Her bag knocks my elbow again and I realise the phone's a clever trick. It means I cannot talk to her, and she can act distracted and distant while carrying out her evil plans.

'Maybe she's buying loads less food than me,' I think, but what folly! She has roughly the same number of items in her bag as I do in mine. I cannot explain it, but what sweeps over me is the feeling that at any second, some kind of major injustice might take place. One that I need to address, head on, right now, lest future generations of Wallaces somehow suffer.

And so I pretend I'm shifting about on my feet, and I gently hit her handbag with my elbow. I sniff and look straight ahead.

'Good!' I think. 'Well *done*, Danny! You just hit a woman's bag! You are marking your territory! She must feel quite the fool! If she wasn't invading your space, there is no *way* her handbag would have been almost imperceptibly glanced by your elbow!'

This might be just two people in a queue, but this has become a mighty battle of wills – a war between all that is right and all that is wrong – and it is I and I alone standing at the gates between one minor slight in the queue-munity, and outright supermarket-based anarchy. In many ways, I am doing this for you.

But I have made my stand. I can relax. Although I'm so relaxed I haven't moved forward quickly enough and the cashier at the till wants to know who's next.

'Oh!' I say, surprised.

'You were before me!' says the queue woman, full of friend-liness.

'Oh, thank you!' I say, pathetically grateful. 'Are you sure? Thanks a lot!'

Yeah. I showed *her*. And I'd do it all again in a *heartbeat*.

Bafta

Deep inside the bowels of a posh Mayfair hotel, another man in black tie strides up to me and slaps me on the back.

'Congratulations!' he says. 'And good *luck*!'

He gives me a double thumbs-up as he backs away, his eyebrows raised, and I raise *my* eyebrows and make a little 'fingers crossed!' face. We chuckle.

There's an awards do on tonight, and for much of the evening, men have been slapping me on the back, or offering sincere handshakes, and looking me deep in the eye and saying, 'I hope you get it!'

'Thank you!' I reply. 'And the best of luck to *you*, as well!'

I am not actually nominated for anything. I didn't even enter. But it is nice to have these men's congratulations and wishes of good luck all the same. And it's easier to take them than to explain why I shouldn't. Although, annoyingly, it has started to make me feel like I might be in with a chance.

Several years earlier, I'd been invited to a different awards bash at the same hotel. This one, I was pleased to note, featured a small novelty photo stand, like the ones where they make you dress up as a Victorian or a Cowboy in a fancy frock or a tiny hat so your friends can make fun of you when they come round after school. But this one was a novelty BAFTA stand. You could have your photo taken with a novelty *BAFTA*! Stick it on your wall! Impress your friends! I watched, as groups of happy pals took to a huge red sofa, holding novelty BAFTAs, and taking novelty photos.

'That looks fun,' I thought. 'Maybe I want *my* photo taken with a novelty fake BAFTA.'

I turned to my friend.

'Shall we have our photo taken with a novelty fake BAFTA?' I said.

'No,' said my friend.

'Come on! It'll be fun! We can pretend we've won BAFTAs!'

'I don't want to,' he said, which was ridiculous, because everyone wants their picture taken with a novelty fake BAFTA. It's like claiming you don't want your picture taken with Mr T.

'Okay,' I said, because I know how his mind works. 'I dare you to go and sit on that massive sofa, all on your own, with a novelty fake BAFTA, and have your picture taken, all lonely, looking like a small angry child.'

'Okay,' he said, and he went and did it.

I ordered another drink, and when I turned round, he was back.

'Where's the photo?' I asked.

'Dunno. Your turn. Get yours done with a celebrity.'

'Eh?'

'That girl from *EastEnders* is over there. Or him.'

He pointed. At Alan Yentob. Alan Yentob, the BBC's then Head of Everything.

'I'm not sure Alan Yentob would have his picture taken with a novelty fake BAFTA. It would be like Simon Bates endorsing video piracy.'

'He's right there. I did *mine*. And *I* looked like a grumpy schoolboy.'

He had a point. Plus, a shot of me and Alan both holding a fake BAFTA would somehow make the fake BAFTA less...*fake*. Maybe it would equate to winning an *actual* BAFTA. I dunno – maybe there's a *rule*.

'Mr Yentob, I was just wondering if I might trouble you for a picture?'

I was holding the fake BAFTA in my hand and he looked delighted by it.

'Of course!' he said. 'Of course!'

Suddenly, we were looking down the lens of the camera.

'Bit closer, boys,' said the photographer, and now I had my arm around him. My arm, around Alan Yentob; two men together, united by a BAFTA. The photographer was getting really into it now, and me and Alan looked at each other and smiled, and at the end, as he was walking away, he turned around and said, '*Congratulations*, by the way!'

'Ha ha ha!' I said, and I pointed at him, as if to say, 'Good one, Alan!'

'So where do I pick up the photos?' I asked the photographer.

'They're all going to the presses,' he said, which was weird, because these were digital, and didn't *need* to go to presses, but then, with a growing ache in my stomach, I realised what he'd *actually* said… 'They're all going to the press.'

Because this was not a novelty fake BAFTA stand. This was a *real* BAFTA stand, for *real* BAFTA winners, and I'd just walked up, grabbed one and forced Alan Yentob to have his picture taken with it. I was a fraud! Two weeks later, a picture of Alan Yentob and 'one of his delighted BAFTA-winning team' made it to the newsstands. *This* was the real scandal at the BBC that no one ever talks about!

So I suppose that actually, I *do* deserve congratulations, after all…

Rookies

I am in a café with two men.

One is as exhausted as me. He is shell-shocked, with hollow eyes.

A waitress asks him if he'd like to order anything else, and it is a full second before he jolts to life, and asks if he can just have more sugar – any sugar at all – for his tea.

She points, shaken but not showing it, at the bowl in front of him, which is overflowing with packet upon packet of fine, free sugar. It is another second before he makes the connection.

'Where's your wife?' he eventually asks me, shaking out a sachet in front of him.

'She's at "Sparky Songs with Richard",' I say. 'Baby Bounce isn't till tomorrow.'

He nods a mournful understanding. He knows that she is at 'Sparky Songs with Richard' despite feeling anything but sparky.

The other man sits silently opposite and smirks. He sees our pain. Because he has been there before. Done it before. Possibly designed and marketed his own T-shirt based on it before.

He is Nick, and he is a father of two.

'It will get better, lads,' he says, finally. 'I promise you.'

But we cannot believe what he says. Even though we know he has experience. Even though we met through a legitimate North London baby group. We simply cannot see the light.

'How can this get better?' I want to say to him. 'How can life ever be the same again? Our miniature boss woke from his slumber nine times last night! Nine! If by getting better you mean he might only wake up *eight* times then yes, I suppose that is marginally better, but it's still eight times more than any sane person hoping to stay sane might choose for themselves.'

Now I would grab him by the collar if I could. I would stand and make a series of impassioned faces.

'He woke up at 7.30 p.m.!' I would yell. 'And at 8.30! Then at 10! And 11! And 2.30! And 3.30! And 3.38! And at 3.48! And just when we were thinking we were tricking our weary bodies into thinking we were getting the best night's sleep of our ruddy lives, he woke up at 5!'

I would now shake him a little.

'Five!' it would be great to shout, but the problem is, I don't even have the energy to *whisper* it, and also, I've *totally* lost my train of thought. Why am I saying five?

Also, who are you and why am I writing things down?

'But what you need to know,' he says, getting us back on track, and it's then that I notice his soft Irish brogue, and for some reason I'm relaxed by it, and soothed, and I wish he'd just keep talking so maybe I could sneak in a subtle four minutes of kip, 'is that it might well get *worse* before it gets better.'

We both look at Nick, charmed by his calm, but then process the words and almost have a seizure. Why the hell did he tell us *that*?

I pull myself together.

'Thank you, Nick,' I say, quite quietly. 'You tell it like it is. And as men in a similar situation, we can take that.'

But this is like a challenge to him.

'Oh, you *want* me to tell it like it is?'

I decide I probably don't.

'Actually, no,' I say.

'Well, I'm *going* to.'

And he does.

And in that moment, we realise that we are nought but soldiers, hunkered down in the baby-battlefield. We are under heavy and sustained fire. I understand my friend's shell-shock. And I understand we need each other.

We are the Dads' Army. And we will be back.

Pickpockets

I am in a cab on my way to an area of London I've never visited before, to visit Colin in his nursery.

I have already made a terrible error with the cabbie, by saying 'Nice work!' when he told me he'd saved me a few minutes on my journey by taking a shortcut he knew. Now, thinking I am deeply fascinated, he is telling me of every single decision he is making, and expecting constant praise in return.

'Gonna turn left here,' he says. 'Avoid the high street.'

'Sounds great!' I reply.

'I can take a right after that,' he says. 'Go round the park.'

'Excellent!' I say.

'Keep your eye out round here,' he says, conspiratorially, as we pull up outside Colin's, and then he turns round and says: 'Lotta pickpockets.'

I *knew* I wouldn't like Colin's new area. I tip the man for keeping me safe.

Inside Colin's new room, I take a look around me.

'Well, this isn't so bad,' I say.

'I am a thirty-three-year-old man living in a nursery,' he says, annoyed.

'Yes,' I say, taking in the wallpaper, with its little teddy bears holding their tiny balloons. 'But it could be worse.'

'How, Dan?' he says. 'How could it be worse?'

'You could be sleeping in a Moses basket,' I try. 'But instead – look! You've got your own little bed!'

We both look at his little bed.

'It's the only one that would fit in here,' he says. 'I have to move that suitcase to the end of it every night just so I've got somewhere to put my feet.'

I try and think of something nice to say. But I can't, so I say, 'Let's go out!'

Colin has his bags with him as he's some work to do in town later, and I stand with them, protectively, in case of pickpockets, as he comes out of the café with the coffees and sandwiches.

'So anyway,' I say. 'It's like he wanted constant praise for every decision he was making. It was exhausting. I had to keep saying, "terrific!" and "wow!" every time he told me he was turning left or right.'

'It's a scam, Dan,' he says. 'He was instilling in you a sense of trust. Making you aware of his expertise and your ineptitude. Making you feel unstreetwise and lost. He was gunning for a tip using the power of fear.'

Colin is scaring me.

'The greatest trick the devil ever played,' he says, eyebrows raised, 'was convincing the world he doesn't exist.'

It is a great quote, but it's not really relevant, so I ignore it.

'Let's sit over there,' I say, and I pick up Colin's bags and start to move off.

But then...

'Hey! What are you *doing?*'

I turn and look. There are two angry men staring at me. I look back at them, confused.

'What?' I say, defensively, shifting Colin's bags further over my shoulder to look businesslike. Maybe they are pickpockets, and this is a trick!

'Gimme my bag back!' says the first man, and I'm confused.

'I haven't—'

And then I realise. I *do* have this man's bag. On my shoulder. I thought it was one of Colin's. But it was this man's bag, and now I've picked it up and accidentally *tried to walk off with it.*

'Oh!' I say. 'I wasn't trying to steal your bag!' But that just somehow makes it worse.

'Put it down!' he says, and now a couple of people have turned round to see what the fuss is about.

'Which one is it?' I say, but when I look at them I realise it's not the Tesco bag or the dirty Puma one, so it's probably the very expensive Italian leather one.

I hand it over, and apologise.

'Yeah, nice try, mate,' he says, opening it slightly, to check the contents.

'I wasn't trying to steal your bag,' I say, again. 'Though you should be careful of pickpockets around here.'

'Why did you say that about pickpockets?' says Colin, when we're far enough away. 'There are no pickpockets around here! Don't embarrass me in my new area.'

'The cabbie made me afraid, Colin!' I say. 'He used the power of fear to gain his tip!'

Colin just shakes his head. He will probably laugh at me, later, alone in his nursery.

After lunch, I hail a cab and get in.

'Gonna try and avoid the high street,' says the driver.

'Nice one,' I say, and a moment later, in the rear-view mirror, I see his eyes light up.

Girls and Boys

I am having a lovely walk in the park, pushing my happy six-month-old son around in his buggy, to give my wife a rest from his constant baby-based demands.

'Okay,' I'd said, leaving the house. '*You* should have a big glass of wine!'

This was to my wife, not my baby.

'Or have a nap. Or a bath. But don't just read baby books and panic because he can't make sandwiches yet, when the baby book says that by now he should be making sandwiches.'

My wife, exhausted, nods. I am breaking no new ground when I say that having a baby is tiring. I am trying to be relaxed about it, as men are prone to do. My wife, on the other hand, has decided to collect and memorise every baby bible ever written.

'No books!' I say, as I close the gate. 'Just rest!'

She nods again, wearily, and pretends she's agreeing, but really, I know she's off to order some more books on-line.

My son has just dropped off to sleep, and I push him away from the noise of a football match, and on, towards a bench, where I get a book out and read. A proper book, too, which never once mentions weaning or nipples.

And then a lady approaches me.

'Aw,' she says, peering over the handle of the buggy. 'How old?'

'Six months,' I say, proudly.

'That's a lovely age,' she says, and we just beam at each other for a second, which isn't something you normally do with strangers unless there's a baby within five feet.

'Teething yet?'

'Yes!' I say. 'Lots of drool!'

She ha-has and as she moves away she gives my son a little wave, and then says, 'Your daddy's very proud of his little girl!'

I smile, about to say thank you, and then I freeze as I take in what she's just said. I look at my son. Yes. This is definitely my son. But this is not the first time this has happened. At least once a week he is mistaken for a little girl by a stranger. I don't know what to do. Is six months too young to get a manly tattoo? I saw a burly little girl-baby recently with two giant earrings – perhaps those vast gold hoops they'd clipped to her ears were because she was always being mistaken for a boy!

I want to shout after these people who mistake him for a her. I want to shout, *'He's just got pretty eyes!'*, but this is not the done thing. I want to teach my son to be a proud metrosexual, but even a proud metrosexual would worry they were a little *too* proud if they were being mistaken for a woman six times an hour.

I look at him again. He's wearing little jeans, a pirate hoodie and a hat with a black-and-white football on. He is definitely a little boy. All I can think is, if people are mistaking him for a little girl, they must be mistaking him for one of those *lesbian* babies you hear so much about.

I read my book a bit more, but I'm distracted, so I take him home.

'I'm sorry,' says my wife, on the sofa, with a baby book I realise I've not seen before. 'I was just about to have a bath, but then—'

'He was mistaken for a little girl again!' I say.

My wife smiles. She quite likes this.

'He's going to get a complex!' I say.

'I don't think babies get complexes,' she says. 'They are not the most complex of people.'

'Well, we don't know that. What do your books say? There must be a chapter in one of your sixteen hundred books that covers baby complexes.'

'I think a baby complex is just a big prison full of babies.'

'That's disgusting,' I say, though I'm not sure why. 'Anyhow, we need to work out how our baby can Man Up.'

My wife looks at me, pityingly.

'He's just got pretty eyes,' she says.

I look at him. He does. He *does* just have pretty eyes. He looks up at me with his big, pretty eyes, and I melt.

'Hey, you know what he'd look good in?' I say, suddenly excited. 'Two huge gold clip-on earrings.'

My wife goes back to reading her book. I go upstairs and have a bath, pleased I no longer feel I have to tattoo my baby.

Alfonso

I'm in Los Angeles for work, and quite by chance I've bumped into an old friend on the street. It would be crazy not to stop and chat, although she seems in quite a hurry.

'I've got time for a quick coffee, though,' she says, and we push through the doors of the nearest Starbucks and start to queue.

'Let's get takeaway cups,' she says, and I look around, glad to be somewhere I feel I know. 'I'm supposed to be meeting my sister round the corner soon but she's not texted me to tell me where yet.'

'Yes, sir?' says the barista, and I wonder why we have to call them baristas these days. 'What would you like?'

'Two large takeaway coffees, please,' I say, and then I remember where I am, and try and translate. 'I mean, two *venti* coffees.'

'Skinny,' says my friend, politely.

'Yes,' I say. 'Two *skinny* venti coffees. White ones.'

He stares at me blankly. My eyes reach for the translation menu again.

'Lattes,' I say, apologetically. 'Two skinny venti *lattes*.' He nods, and begins to work.

'I hate that,' I whisper to my friend. 'Why can't I just have a white coffee? Why do I have to learn a whole new language? Doesn't matter where in the world you are. London. Tokyo. Paris. Here. You can't just speak English, or Japanese, or French. You have to speak *Starbucks* too.'

There's a beep-beep from her jacket. I continue on.

'No other company invents its own language,' I say. 'Apart from maybe McDonald's, but you can learn that language just by adding 'Mc' to things. A moron can crack that code. McChicken! McNuggets! Even then, they don't apply it to coffee. You don't ask for a McCoffee, do you, not unless you're odd?'

But she is distracted by her phone and my words have fallen on deaf ears, which is a pity, because I think they are very perceptive and deserve a wider audience.

'Your name?' asks the barista, just as my friend looks up.

'Sorry?' I say.

'Name?'

It's busy here. They're taking names to avoid you nicking someone else's order.

'It's Alfonso,' I say.

He gives me a quizzical glance and I smile to acknowledge the lie, then he scribbles on the cups. I've only said it to make my friend laugh, but also it feels like I'm making a stand, somehow.

'Why did you say *Alfonso*?' she giggles.

'If they can do it, I can,' I say, of my stupid joke. 'I am merely contributing to their own, made-up language. From now on, "Alfonso" is Starbucks for "Danny". And what's more, it applies to *all* Dannys, not just this one. If they ever try to call me Danny I will simply stare at them blankly until they call me Alfonso.'

But then her phone beep-beeps.

'Oh, no…' she says. 'She's parked round the corner.'

'Eh?'

'My sister. She's parked where she shouldn't be and she wants me to come before she gets a ticket.'

I hope she is not making this up because she didn't like my gentle observational humour about the Starbucks naming system. I suppose I *was* making fun of their language, and that *is* a bit like racism.

'Do you want to wait for your coffee?' I say.

'I can't…do you want to come with me?'

I look at her. I look at the baristas busily making their coffees. It seems rude to abandon them now, so full of beans.

She nods her understanding and says, 'Bye, Dan,' then turns on her heel, and for a moment I consider calling out after her that within *these* walls my name is *not* Dan, but Alfonso, but it's quite a crowded place, and also, I don't really want people thinking that's true.

And then…

'Alfonso?' says a man at the other end of the counter, quite loudly, and placing two coffees down.

Brilliant.

I leave it a moment.

'Alfonso?' says the man, louder, looking around, and this time other people hear.

The original barista looks over at me, smiles, and points at the coffees. My joke's backfired and he knows it. I only found this funny before, in front of my friend. Now being a man named Alfonso seems odd and unalluring.

'Have conviction!' I think. 'You were making a point! Make your stand against the homogenisation of our culture, right here, in front of these people! Have Alfonso stuck up there on the board, next to the ventis and grandes and skinnys! *That'd* show 'em!'

But in the end I decide it is easier not to be a man of conviction, so, smiling, I quietly grab both of Alfonso's venti skinny lattes and I leg it.

Mike's Way

It's lunchtime in America and we're hungry.

'How about there?' says my wife, pointing at a place we've never noticed before. It's called Mike's, and according to the window display it specialises in sandwiches 'Mike's Way', which is lucky, seeing as Mike seems to be the man making them.

'Yes?' says the man inside, who may or may not be Mike.

My wife orders the American Classic, and I approve, because anything with Classic in the title must be terrific.

'And do you want it Mike's Way?' says the man, and I am instantly wary. I have warned my wife about this. When Americans ask you if you'd like something 'their' way, it can lead to a very unusual sauce, or the whole thing arriving in a giant onion ring.

She says yes, and I cast her a glance that says *'Are you sure?'* I decide to make a point.

'I will have the Veggie,' I say.

'Mike's Way?' says the man.

'No,' I say, and he looks up at me. 'No, not Mike's Way. But could I have some jalapeño peppers?'

I turn and look at my wife, proudly. I have been clever. Not only have I rejected Mike's Way, but I have in addition ordered *jalapeño peppers*, making *this* sandwich *Danny's Way*. She hides her pride well.

Back in the car, my wife opens her sandwich. It is fantastic. Ham and cheese and crisp, fresh lettuce, with onions and tomatoes leaning from either side. It looks healthy and good. I decide to give her this one. She took a risk but she got away with it. I unwrap my Veggie sandwich. And I stare at it.

There is one slice of cheese and about forty jalapeños.

'Can this be right?' I say. 'It's just a jalapeño sandwich! But I ordered a Veggie! What *is* this?'

My wife turns and looks at me, very seriously.

'It's because you made a point of not having it Mike's Way,' she says. 'You've insulted Mike. You had the chance to have it Mike's Way, and you chose to rebuff him. Mike probably doesn't like it when people rebuff Mike's Way. That's why you got a jalapeño sandwich.'

'But I don't want a jalapeño sandwich! *No one* does! And I didn't rebuff it! Not exactly! I just wanted vegetables! There are no vegetables in this veggie sandwich! Just more jalapeños than any human has ever had in a sandwich before!'

I glance longingly at my wife's sub.

'Right, I'm taking it back,' I say. 'I obviously confused them with the jalapeños. Somehow he thought I wanted jalapeños in place of standard vegetables.'

My wife just shrugs and I get out of the car and stride purposefully back into the shop.

'Hello,' I say, inside. 'I think there's been some confusion. I wanted a Veggie sandwich with jalapeños but this appears to be just a jalapeño sandwich without vegetables.'

The man stares at me.

'You don't want jalapeños?'

'Just a Veggie sandwich,' I say, staying strong. 'Forget the jalapeños.'

'And you want *this* one Mike's Way?'

And this, I realise, is where I have to be a man. Because if I have it Mike's Way, I am conceding that I am totally at fault. But I am *not* to blame. So I say…

'No, *not* Mike's Way.'

It is tense. I turn and stare out at the car park, where I see my wife happily crumpling up her sandwich wrapper.

'Finally,' I say, back in the car. I unwrap my new sandwich. And I sigh.

Because this one is just some cheese and four thin slices of green pepper.

This is *worse* than the other one!*

What's going *on*?

'You should've had it Mike's Way,' says my wife. 'Mike's Way has vegetables.'

'But you should get vegetables the *normal* way!' I plead. 'It's a Veggie sandwich! Why is it just random peppers?! I tell you what's happened here. Mike has *stolen* the standard way of doing things! He's claimed anything standard or normal is *his* way! Like he *invented* it! The arrogance!'

My wife quietly starts the car.

'Mike apparently thinks only *he* knows how to do things! He thinks we don't know what we want! "Oh, I'll have a Coke please, Mike. Do I want it Mike's Way? No. Why not just pop a pepper in a cup?"'

We reverse away from Mike's.

'"A Margherita pizza, Mike's Way?" No thanks, Mike! I'll just have it the way you think everyone else has it. Just hand me a chicken and a whistle.'

'You shouldn't have annoyed Mike,' says my wife, shaking her head.

I scowl as we leave the parking lot.

'Mike has not seen the last of me,' I vow, plotting my revenge.

---

* *figs 2a and 2b, appendix*

The Phone

'Hello, I'm calling from room 264…the phone in my room doesn't seem to be working.'

'Oh, but you're calling from room 264?'

'Yes. I'm calling you from room 264, but from my mobile. The phone in my room doesn't seem to be working, you see.'

'So…I'm sorry I don't understand.'

'I'm calling from my mobile. My mobile works, that's not the problem. The problem is the phone in the room.'

'What room are you in?'

'I'm in room 264.'

'And the phone isn't working?'

'That's correct.'

'And you're calling from your mobile, but that works?'

'Yes. But the phone in the room does not.'

'Oh. Okay. Well…shall I try it?'

'Yes, sure, you can try it, but it isn't working.'

'I'll try it, just in case it's fine.'

'It isn't, but okay, try it.'

'I'll try it.'

Holding music

'Hello? Mr Wallace? Your phone seems to be working fine.'

'What do you mean?'

'I rang it, and I could hear the ring tone, although at this point no one picked up.'

'No, I know no one picked up. I'm right here. And it didn't ring.'

'I could hear the ring tone, sir, but no one picked up. Is there anyone in the room who could've picked up?'

'*I'm* in the room.'

'And you didn't pick up?'

'You know I didn't pick up. If I'd picked up, I'd've said hello.'

'But…you're in the room right now?'

'Yes.'

'Shall I ring it again?'

'It's not working.'

'Let me just try it again.'

Holding music

'Yeah, it's ringing, but no one's picking up, sir.'

'That's because it's *not* ringing.'

'And you're calling from your mobile?'

'Yes.'

'But you're in the room currently?'

'Yes!'

'Would you like me to connect you to the room?'

'Eh?'

'Would you like me to connect you to the room, so you can see if it's working?'

'Why would I want you to connect me to the room? If you connect me to the room, I'd be talking to myself on the phone, and you'd be gone!'

'It's not a problem to connect you.'

'But I don't want to talk to myself! I can do that without paying! And anyway, I can't talk to myself, because the phone in the room doesn't work!'

'Well, it seems to be working fine, sir. It's just that no one's picking up, so it goes to voicemail. Are you sure you're in room 262?'

'264.'

'Yes, that's what I'm ringing, 264. And you definitely can't hear the phone ringing when I ring it? Because it rings and then it goes to voicemail.'

'I promise you, if I heard it ringing, I would definitely pick up. This is not a mind game. I'm not trying to get extra voicemails.'

'Well, I'm not sure what to do. Let me ask my colleague.'

'Wait—'

Holding music

'Hello, Mr Wallace? I hear your phone isn't working?'

'That's right.'

'Seems to be working now, loud and clear.'

'No, this is my mobile.'

'Well, have you tried calling your mobile company about it? Perhaps from the phone in your room?'

'No, it's the phone in the room that doesn't work!'

'I see. Let me just connect you...'

Holding music

Ringtone

'Hello. The person in the room is unable to take your call right now. Please leave your message after the tone'.

Beeeep

'Um...hello. It's me. I don't think my phone is working.'

Cough

Click

The Study

I arrive back in the country to the wonderful news that my friend Steve has taken an interest in a new girl at work. The last time he took an interest in a girl this way, he sprayed himself with Sainsbury's Grapefruit and Lime room spray in order to secure her attentions, as he did not feel confident enough in his own scent and didn't have any deodorant.

Confusingly, it did not work.

'I have learnt my lesson,' he says, very seriously, as we rattle about on the tube. 'Women do not like men who smell of fruit, no matter the combination. That's scientific *fact*. Instead, women rely…on *pheromones*.'

He looks at me wisely, and I have to wonder whether perhaps he is somehow related to Colin.

'Please say you've not bought pheromones off the internet,' I say.

Steve once bought pheromones off the internet. It was a last-ditch attempt to secure a lady at a Christmas party.

Confusingly, it did not work.

'I have not bought pheromones off the internet,' he says, matter-of-factly. 'And anyway, that would've worked if I'd put enough on.'

'You put it *all* on.'

'Well, I'll be relying on my *own* pheromones this evening,' he says, as we step off the tube. 'One hundred per cent Steve. Hey, that's not a bad name for a brand, actually.'

I consider it. There is a type of pheromone you can buy which is made up of a substance released by lactating female dogs to calm puppies. Perhaps this is what he intends to release, although I hope not literally. I hope he will not be milking a dog in front of some girls.

I'm to be Steve's wingman for the first few minutes of a casual drink with this girl, and then I'm going to make my excuses and leave. It is an elegant plan, which relies on Steve's own natural personality, wit and charm rather than internet-bought pheromones or room spray. Which makes me hope he's brought some room spray.

She is waiting at a table as we arrive, and Steve is instantly wonderful. She laughs – *giggles*, even – and when I return from the bar, she seems smitten with him. She is touching her hair and doing all the things you read about in lady magazines.

And then she says something completely innocuous about work.

'Actually, I totally disagree with you,' says Steve, sternly, and there is an icy moment. Steve launches into a passionate monologue about why this girl is wrong, what a great place to work they share, how people should be more appreciative of their surroundings. He shakes his head, and harrumphs, and grumpily taps the table as he makes his point. The girl looks ashamed, and starts to backtrack, and says how *welcome* everyone's made her feel, and how she honestly didn't mean anything by it.

'He's blowing it!' I think. 'He *had* her, and now he's blowing it!'

I attempt to interrupt.

'Well,' I say. 'No one's office is perfect. And I'm sure that—'

'Let's change the subject,' says Steve. And then he's his old self again, and tells a funny story about ships. The girl melts slightly, grateful to have been given a reprieve. She walks to the bathroom moments later.

'This is going brilliantly!' says Steve. 'You can go in a minute!'

'This is going *terribly*!' I say. 'What are you *doing*?'

And he just looks at me like a master might look upon his naive apprentice. Which is when it hits me.

Steve's read a survey.

'Oh, God…you've read some kind of report, haven't you?' I say. 'Some kind of scientific report which tells you to be all weird with women.'

'I have, sir!' he says. 'You have to be all nice, then take issue with something they say so that they can see you are strong-minded and independent, and then be all nice again. It makes them like you!'

'What if it doesn't?' I say. 'What if it makes them think you're emotionally unstable?'

'Then I'm a project! A project ripe for development! But an opinionated one, who knows his own mind! *Science*, Dan!'

I shake my head at him, then realise he's doing the same to me.

'This is like the room spray all over again!' I protest. 'This is one hundred per cent Steve!'

'*Thank* you,' he says, meaning it. 'Hang on, heads up…'

The girl takes her seat, unsurely.

'…and that's why I think you're wrong,' he says, pretending he's just told me off for something.

I decide it is time for me to leave.

In the morning, I lie in bed hoping that Steve has learnt his lesson. That science will never take the place of chemistry.

My phone beeps. A text from Steve. I read it, and blink.

Confusingly, it's worked.

The Mumbler

There is a workman in my house, and there is a problem, because he is a mumbler.

I can make out a good deal of what he is saying, and that's fine, because so far, a good deal is all I've needed.

But now he's taken his mumbling to a whole new level. He's mumbling so much, and with such veracity, that I'm not certain if he's just mumbling, or if he's mumbling *at* me.

Sometimes, he's mumbled at the work a previous workman has done, and this type of mumble generally means I should frown, and make a face, which implies I agree with his mumble. He has mumbled at something and then turned to me, wide-eyed and grinning, which implies that I should probably share the apparent mirth of his mumble.

But now he's looking at me after having mumbled something that can only be a question. A question that requires an answer. I am raised from mere mumblee to mumble-*respondent*.

I balk. And do the only thing I *can* do, which is to ask him to repeat himself.

'Sorry?' I say.

Without blinking, he mumbles it once again, and now I am nervous. Because I know the rules of talking to people who mumble. You cannot anger their kind. These people do not *know* they are mumblers. And *non*-mumblers cannot *tell* mumblers they are mumblers. Non-mumblers are polite. They enunciate. Unlike mumblers, with their scant regard for the boundaries of society, and their mumbling.

'God, I'm *so* sorry, could you say that one more time?' I plead, even *more* politely this time, because I know how close to the edge I am sailing. I *have* to hear him this time, he has to rise up above the mumble, because not to do so would put us in a terrifying area of social convention.

I see a moment of annoyance in his eyes. Just a slither.

And he repeats himself. And yet once more he mumbles.

He stares at me now, his eyes expectant, searching me for an answer. And yet all I've heard is the kind of dulled noise you hear from the people who live two doors away, when one of them's done something the other doesn't like.

I realise, with a shudder, that this is where the rule of three comes in. You can ask someone to repeat themselves once. You can feign a hearing problem and ask them once more. But the third time – that's your last shot.

'I...am *so* sorry,' I say, moving closer, and cupping my hand to my ear, implying that this is entirely my fault and I've never been so rude in my life. 'Just...what was that again?'

After this, I am out. After this, there's nothing more I can do. It is *imperative* I translate this mumble.

I catch his eyes darting to the right for just a moment. He's probably swearing in his head. Or maybe he mumbled it and I just didn't hear.

'Affm mffm mmom,' he says, splaying his hands out in front of him and raising his eyebrows.

I stare at him.

I have absolutely no idea what 'affm mffm mmom' means.

So I say, 'Whatever you think.'

I'm relieved. And then this relief is replaced by panic. What if he's just told me he needs to replace all the wiring? What if he's just said he needs to knock down the whole house and start again? That could cost me hundreds!

And then: suspicion. What if this 'mumbling' is just a scam? What if this 'mumbling' is a way of securing additional, unnecessary work? What if this 'mumbler' is using my middle-class embarrassment as a means of bankrupting me and getting his own way?

God, that's *brilliant*, I think. I have a newfound respect for this evil genius.

Later that evening, my wife returns and asks me to put the washing on. I mumble a response. She frowns and asks me again.

'Affm mffm mmom' I say.

'Why are you mumbling?' she says.

'Affm mffm mmom,' I shrug.

'You're not even saying anything. Those aren't even words.'

I take a breath. Rule of three. Remember, Dan: rule of three.

'Affm mffm mmom.'

I splay my hands out, and raise my eyebrows. Genius.

There is a pause.

'So are you going to put the washing on, or not?'

This is *unheard* of. She can't do that! We've done the rule of three! We've pushed past the normal areas of politeness and acceptability!

I want to tell my wife how proud I am of her, and how impressed, but in the end I just mumble a Yes and put the washing on.

Lunch

It's lunchtime, so I stop working and wander downstairs to see what's going on.

'What's going on?' I say to my wife, who's cooking something brilliant.

'Salmon, tomato and onion!' she says, proudly. 'With cous cous.'

I am amazed. Since we had a kid, we've hardly ever eaten anything proper for lunch, let alone anything proper with cous cous. We've mainly eaten Super Noodles, at a table covered in bibs.

And amazingly, my wife hasn't finished.

'After that,' she says, delighted, 'pear with cinnamon for dessert!'

Wow!

'I just have to purée it all,' she says.

Something about that sentence makes me realise this is probably not for me. We're both busy people, but not so busy that we can't chew our food.

'And…what shall *we* have?' I try, lightly, casting a jealous glance at my son. Maybe we can have some of his salmon, tomato and onion, too.

'I think there's some Super Noodles in the cupboard,' she says, distractedly. 'If you want Super Noodles?'

Of course I want Super Noodles. Who doesn't want Super Noodles?

I eye the salmon, tomato and onion as I trudge over to the cupboard and open the door.

Inside, I move fresh vegetables and healthy baby pastas out of the way and find a packet of Super Noodles, but it's Southern Fried Chicken flavour, so I suppose that's a result.

When I turn round, my wife is holding an unusual packet. It says 'Quinoa'. I decide not to say anything because I'm not sure how to pronounce it, but still – quinoa. My child is eating quinoa. Why aren't *I* eating quinoa?

I am a second-class citizen in my own home, I realise. I am the underclass, forced to scrabble around in cupboards, foraging for Southern Fried Chicken-flavour Super Noodles like a member of Fagin's gang, while a fat little aristocrat gorges himself on cous cous and quinoa.

Still, at least my wife is in this with me. We are together. United by the Friday-night-aftertaste of Southern Fried Chicken. I look at her, fondly.

'Do you want Super Noodles too?' I ask. 'I think there's some Barbecue Beef flavour in there too?'

But my wife smiles at me, with kindness in her eyes, and softly shakes her head, as if to say, '*You* have them, darling. You deserve them.'

I make a face that says, 'I take your point,' and quietly escort my Super Noodles through to the lounge.

When I am finished, I take my bowl back into the kitchen and notice that my son has hardly touched his pear and cinnamon dessert. This, I imagine, will disillusion my wife. It must be tough on her, eating badly, but seeing good, hearty food go to waste at the hands of this little dictator. She is standing by the oven, and flips it open, and as she turns, I see what she's taken out.

'What's...what's *that*?' I say, shocked, and staring at the plate she's holding.

'This?' she says. 'It's...a pie.'

'A pie?' I say. 'You're having a pie?'

She's having a pie! But it's not *just* a pie. It's a pie with *vegetables*. A side dish!

'There are vegetables on your plate!' I say, alarmed. 'Where did this pie come from?'

'The neighbours brought it round,' she says.

'Just one bit?' I say. 'They just brought one bit of pie?'

'I had the other bit last night,' she says, quietly.

I think back to what I'd had last night.

Super Noodles!

'I didn't think you'd want any…' says my wife, shrugging, and jabbing at a carrot with her fork.

'You didn't think I'd want any *delicious pie*?' I say. 'You thought you'd say, "Do you want some delicious pie?" and I'd say, "I'm okay for pie, thanks."'

I have caught her out! I have caught her trying to better herself! This shameful attempt to break out of the underclass and join the fat little aristocrat who eats salmon and shuns his dessert! I never, ever took this woman for a social climber.

'Well, well,' I say, shaking my head to show my disappointment. 'And how do you propose to make this up to me?'

She points at my son's now-cold pear and cinnamon, which is starting to darken and congeal, and she raises her eyebrows, hopefully.

I carry it back upstairs and eat it quietly on my own.

You've got to take what you can get sometimes.

The Wedding

We are at a wedding of a friend of my wife's, somewhere outside Edinburgh, where we know only a very few people.

The ceremony is over, and we are at our table, surrounded by a dozen strangers, when the speeches begin.

It is clear that while this is a day of happiness and joy, there is something bittersweet in the air. The groom's grandmother is not here. She passed away, only recently.

There has been a lot of talk about her today. About how proud she'd have been. I have been asked several times already by people I've only just met if I knew her, and each time I've felt guilty when I've had to say I don't even know the groom.

So far in the speeches, she's not been mentioned. But now the groom stands up to speak, and everyone knows: this is it.

I take a swig of my wine and glance around the room. There is a sad anticipation. I put my glass down, ready to listen, but the wine's gone down the wrong way, and I have to politely stifle a cough. I get away with it, because the groom has started with a joke, and so my cough is drowned out. But I realise with mounting horror that there is another cough on the way. A *secondary* cough, to finish off the job.

I try and stifle this one, too, but stifling a cough isn't easy. The groom continues his funny speech, and there are more laughs, so I try and time my cough at the same time, but this is a *time bomb*, and eventually, I make the weirdest sound I have ever made.

A kind of *hwuuragh*.

There is a second of silence that lasts an hour, and one or two people look over at me. I try and avoid their eye and pretend this is a totally natural noise for a human to make. Like people are always going *hwuuragh* where I'm from.

The groom is now talking about how much he wishes his grandmother could have been here today.

My wife subtly pushes a glass of water towards me. I try and smile at her, weakly, but my eyes are now streaming from the effort of dealing with the coughs. I can feel two distinct rivers of water on my cheeks, and I look around the room, and all I can think of is, *please don't let me cough again.*

But now I have to blow my nose – there are new rivers taking over my top lip, joining the tears at the side of my mouth, and I hear my wife scrabbling about for a tissue.

I lean to the girl next to me.

'Sorry about my cough,' I say, covering my mouth, and nodding in an I'm-sure-you-understand kind of way. But she doesn't seem to have heard the whole sentence, and says, gently, 'Hey, this kind of stuff always gets *me*, too,' and then she rubs my shoulder in a comforting way. 'Days like this can be tough.'

She turns to watch the groom.

'I'm not grieving,' I want to tell her. 'I was stifling an unruly cough!'

But this would sound odd, and I realise that to get away with this, I'm going to have to pretend I was indeed very sad. I'm going to have to pretend that I'm a very sad man at a stranger's wedding who is crying at the mere mention of an elderly woman he's never even met.

And not just crying, making weird grieving noises, too.

After the speeches, I feel a squeeze on my shoulder. I look up, and it's an older man I've never met before. I think he might be someone's drunken uncle. We stare at each other for a second. He looks at me, like he *understands*, then squeezes my shoulder, pats me on the back, and walks away again.

I look at the girl next to me, and she smiles, sweetly, as if she's just witnessed a special moment.

'Did you know her well?' she says, and I wonder whether I should come clean.

'A lovely woman,' I say, looking sad.

'Dan,' says my wife. 'This is Charlie.'

It's the groom. I stand and shake his hand.

'Nice to meet you, Danny,' he says. 'I wondered if we'd *ever* meet!'

'Ha!' I say. 'Yes!'

'Must be weird, being at a wedding where you know no one!'

'Ha!' I say, again. 'Yes.'

And I sit back down.

The girl looks at me, oddly.

Mystery

I am sitting in my study when a very strange text comes through.

I read it, and read it again, and then have to go downstairs to show my wife.

'The actor Terence Stamp wishes to speak with me,' I say, bewildered.

'Terence Stamp?' she says.

'Terence Stamp,' I say.

'Why?' she says. 'Why does Terence Stamp wish to speak with you?'

I have no idea why Terence Stamp wishes to speak with me. The text, from someone at his agency, simply says, 'Terence Stamp wishes to speak with you. May I give him your mobile number?'

I am immediately nervous. Our paths nearly crossed a couple of years ago when Terence was filming a part in an adaptation of one of my books, but he was gone in an instant and I presumed out of my life forever. I had watched him from afar, admired his work. This was, after all, General Zod from *Superman*. And yet now, Terence Stamp was summoning *me*.

'What are you going to say?' says my wife, confused, reading the text.

'I'm going to ask why Terence Stamp wishes to speak with me,' I say, my voice uncertain. I have a horrible feeling I may be in trouble somehow with Terence Stamp. It feels like the headmaster wants to see me but won't say why.

I send a reply.

'Of course! But do you know why Terence Stamp wants to speak with me?'

My wife and I sit down and stare at the phone. I move it closer to the window so it gets better reception.

Finally, a reply: 'Sorry, no idea. I did ask, but was told it was personal. Thank you.'

I look at my wife, alarmed.

'It's personal!' I say. 'We need to work out exactly how many ways I could have offended the actor Terence Stamp since our paths nearly crossed in 2008!'

We struggle to come up with any, so throw more possibilities out there.

'Maybe he thinks you're the footballer Danny Wallace,' she says. 'Or Danny Glover. That's not unusual.'

I phone Colin from the house phone, not wanting to use my mobile in case the actor Terence Stamp calls up and finds it engaged. That would be just yet another way of offending him.

Colin answers in a very odd way, stating his name and asking how he can be of help. I realise that is how he answers the phone to unusual numbers. I would normally make fun of him for this which would lead to a protracted conversation illuminating me to his human foibles and frailties, which I would then tell *you*, but today there are more pressing matters to be dealt with.

'Terence Stamp wants to speak with me!' I say.

'What? Why?' he says.

'I don't know! All I know is it's personal!'

'When will he be speaking with you?'

'It could happen anytime. He could literally call at any moment. That's why I am speaking to you today from the home phone.'

'Oh!' says Colin, like he's delighted. Using the home phone does seem to be a strange way of complimenting someone these days. Like you're committed to the phone call for the long haul. You want this call to work.

I am at pains to stress that this is not a compliment.

'Ask him what it was like to play General Zod in *Superman*,' says Colin.

'I will not do that,' I say. 'But what do you think he could possibly want?'

'Maybe he wants you to write him a musical or something!' says Colin, out of nowhere, and I decide perhaps Colin is not the best person to ask about these matters.

For four, five, then six hours I potter about the house, checking my mobile reception, making sure the ringer is on, but Terence Stamp does not call. I decide maybe he's in LA, where they're eight hours behind, so as I go to bed that night, I leave my phone on, and for a few moments it lights up a darkened bedroom, until it – and I – fade into blackness.

In the morning, my wife taps my forehead.

'Has Terence Stamp left a message?' she asks.

I check. No. No he has not.

Wait! A text!

But it's from Colin.

'What happened with Terence Stamp?'

I sigh. I carry my phone around the house with me all morning.

'I wonder what Terence Stamp wanted,' says my wife, that afternoon, staring out the window, wistfully, as if a glimpse of a better life has just passed us by.

'I guess we will never know,' I say, sadly.

Collecting

Colin is looking at me with suspicion in his eyes because I have told him I am not a collector, and conventional wisdom dictates, he says, that all men are collectors.

'I just don't,' I say.

'But you *must*,' he says. 'Lawnmowers?'

'I do not collect lawnmowers. You've known me a long time. Surely you'd know if I collected lawnmowers.'

'Comics, then? Or a lock of hair from every woman you meet?'

I take that as a joke, because so long as I do, it means we can still hang out.

'Not really. I save stuff, of course. Stuff that *means* stuff. But I don't "collect" stuff.'

Colin remains silent, willing me on, hoping I'll say something that makes it okay, but the simple truth is, if I *do* tell him of my collection, he'll never let it go. It will be the thing that defines me in his eyes. Years of friendship and shared experience will go out the window as I become the person he introduces to people by telling them what it is I collect, not who I am or how we met.

Because I suppose, if *you* were to ask me what I collect, I would come straight out and say it, and I'd say it like this:

I collect black-and-white photographs of Shropshire table tennis teams from the late 1950s and early '60s.

Now, I realise I am probably in the minority here. There are no clubs the casual collector of black-and-white photographs of

Shropshire table tennis teams from the late 1950s and early '60s can join. There are no clubs the *serious* collector can join, either, because as far as I can tell, it's just me.

Not that I ever meant to collect them. I have little interest in table tennis, though this far outweighs my interest in Shropshire. And I've never been brilliant at collecting, either. As a kid, I gave up collecting stamps after sensibly realising I was never going to be able to collect them *all*.

The simple truth is, one day I had *no* black-and-white photographs of Shropshire table tennis teams from the late 1950s and early '60s, and the next day, I had *three*. The day after that, I had four. And thus, Britain's most extensive private collection of black-and-white photographs of Shropshire table tennis teams from the late 1950s and early '60s was born.

I found them on a market stall. And on this market stall, in a small and damp brown box, were people's *memories*. Bruised, battered, dog-eared photos of weddings, or trips to the beach, or holidays on windswept moors in ill-fitting slacks, or shots of kids with tiny ice creams by dad's new car. Each one, I realised, told a story. And they were stories that would probably never again be told. These were the only pieces of evidence that these events – some small, but some absolutely life-changing – had ever even happened at all, and they were now damp and exposed and vulnerable under the sagging canvas of an East London market stall.

So I bought some. Just to make sure they were safe. Just to make sure someone *had* them. I was saving stuff. Stuff that meant stuff.

'What – so *nothing*?' says Colin. 'You're saying you collect nothing? I find it very odd that you collect nothing, Dan. It's almost like you're being wilfully eccentric. I imagine you're probably thinking about growing a beard.'

I think again about the photos, and I remember the tight tops and short shorts and thick NHS specs and well-worn table tennis paddles...and I remember the reverse sides of the photos, too, because someone had thought to record everyone's names on the back, to guard their memory for the future, just as I hoped to do. Doris Ackland. Shirley Whitebread. Brian Leggett. Peter Hotchkiss. Gordon Upham. The darlings of the late '50s/early '60s Shropshire table tennis scene. And maybe, I thought, if I write some of them down somewhere, just as I've done right here and right now, maybe someone out there might know one of them, and tell them, and I'll be able to give them their photos back. Their memories.

Because even if I only end up with just *one* black-and-white photograph of a Shropshire table tennis team from the late 1950s or early '60s, it's a fair bet to say I'll probably still possess the world's largest and best private collection.

Though before that happens, I decide to tell Colin.

'I collect black-and-white photographs of Shropshire table tennis teams from the late 1950s and early '60s,' I say, and he looks at me.

And he shakes his head, and he says, '*Sometimes* I wish you would take being a man just a *little* more seriously.'

Blacks

An important part of being a grown-up is going to dinner with other grown-ups, and talking about grown-up things.

'Are you ready yet?' I call out to my wife, and she walks into the living room, fixing an earring to her ear.

'You don't have to shout,' she says. 'You've become very loud lately.'

'I have *not* become loud,' I say, loudly. 'And I wasn't shouting. I was calling out. There is a huge difference between shouting and calling out. Calling out is much friendlier than shouting.'

Honestly. She knows I can't abide loud people, loudly bellowing their loud opinions. Why would she lump me in with those? I have made my opinions on these people perfectly clear and yet still she did it. And I haven't said *anything* embarrassing since I said that the baby looked like Hitler.

Half an hour later we are on our way into town, where we are meeting two of her old friends. They are taking us to their regular haunt – a place called Blacks. Its outside is painted entirely black, which is handy as it means it doesn't have to put up a big sign saying 'Blacks'.

Inside, the other male grown-up says 'Shall we order some wine?' and I say 'Yes!' and he says 'Would you like to choose?' and I take the wine list and look at it for a moment, before passing it back and saying '*You* choose!'

My wife nudges me slightly, and it becomes apparent that I must've said '*You* choose!' a little too loudly, because it is quiet here, and dark, and people are talking in murmurs.

I give her a look that says 'it is important to begin an evening in an effusive and gregarious way as this implies you are committed to mutual engagement and fun and anyway it was only two words and *neither* of them were like calling a baby Hitler' but I can tell this simple notion is lost on her.

'So, Danny!' says the male grown-up, quite loudly, and I notice that *his* wife isn't nudging *him* to keep quiet. 'How's tricks?'

'Good,' I say, quietly. 'How about *your* tricks?'

The more I can simply bat his questions back at him the quieter I can seem, and also it implies I am selfless and interested and unlikely to say anything wrong.

Our starters arrive, and soon we are chuckling along, eating unusual meats and talking about grown-up things like grown-ups do. We talk about our babies, about how weird it is to be away from them for an evening, and about house prices and politics and telly. And as the clichés pile up, the stranger it feels being here, in Blacks, drinking wine and talking about babies, when just a year ago, we'd have been in a curry house, or pub.

'Perhaps this is just what happens,' I think. 'As you get older, as your responsibilities become greater, as your time becomes more limited, your nights out become more grown-up, more focused.'

But, as we ride the bus home, I wonder if there's a balance to be struck. Whether we can still do the things we used to do, despite the changes. My wife nestles into me.

'That was nice,' she says, as I stare out of the window, at all the curry houses and pubs that are now passing us by. 'And hey…I'm sorry I told you to be less loud. I've just got a headache. You've *not* started being all loud.'

I give her a thank you squeeze, but she knows something's on my mind.

'What?' she says, as we approach our stop. 'Didn't you have a good time?'

The bus starts to slow and I take my arm from my wife's shoulder. I notice an old man is listening to our conversation.

'It was really lovely…' I say, standing up. 'It's just…'

'What?' she said, as the doors open and we get ready to jump off the bus. 'What is it?'

I think of where we've just been. Of the wine, and the meats, and the conversation, and it strikes me again as the perfect metaphor for grown-up life as it now is. But how to put it?

I know.

'I guess I'm just not all that keen on Blacks,' I say.

Turns out I said that too loud.

Conversation Starters for Ladies and Gentlemen: 2

TOPIC 1

I would like Pearly Kings a lot more if they didn't flaunt their wealth so much on their jackets. Once I followed a row of discarded pearls in the hope that it would lead me to some kind of Aladdin's cave of pearly treasures, but it turned out it was just a fat lad shedding Mentos.

TOPIC 2

Do you know what? They say 'six of one, half a dozen of the other', don't they? But when you really think about it, that's exactly the same thing!

TOPIC 3

If you're worried you're being stalked, follow the person you think is stalking you on Twitter. If they do everything you do but just a minute or so later, you might have a point. Whatever you do, don't write, 'just following my stalker', because then they'd have to get someone to stalk them, too, and three's a crowd, man.

TOPIC 4

There was a nice moment this week while standing in a loud bar talking to a lady I'd just met. Halfway through our conversation, a friendly man stopped and stood with us, and I realised with horror I'd met him before but couldn't remember his name. He was now expecting an introduction, which I just couldn't deliver. Eventually, he wandered off.

'God, I'm so sorry,' I said to the lady. 'I couldn't remember that guy's name so I couldn't introduce you!'

'Oh,' she said. 'That was my husband.'

It seems unlikely she did not mention this to him afterwards.

TOPIC 5

I bought some 'extra long life' batteries and they lasted one week. I had no idea you could buy sarcastic batteries.

After that

Sharing

I am striding down the high street on my way briefly to meet Colin and I am frustrated because there is a person to my left who has started walking at exactly the same speed as me.

It is strangely embarrassing. We are not together. Yet we look like we are together. And neither one of us wants to be the one who slows down.

'Yield!' I want to shout. 'Cease this pointless battle of wills! Find your own speed and space! I have been walking at this pace for ages! This pace is *my* pace!'

Yet the lady continues matching me, stride-for-stride. It is incredibly stressful. Eventually I bowl into the café, pleased I had seen this challenger off and given as good as I got. Yeah, she'll rue the day she messed with me.

'You seem happy,' says Colin, stirring his tea.

'I am, sir!'

But I decide not to tell him why, because that might make me seem petty and childish and it is important no one ever discovers this about me.

'I'm happy too,' he says. 'Woke up feeling like a hundred bucks!'

'Yeah, I'm not sure that's the phrase,' I say. 'Hey, do people sometimes walk at the same pace as you on the street?'

'What?'

'You're walking along or you turn a corner, and suddenly there's someone else there and they seem completely unembarrassed about walking at the same speed as you, right *next* to you?'

Colin stares for a second, shrugs and ignores me.

'I've decided I'm not going to buy any more birthday presents for men,' he says. 'I stop as of now, as should every other man in Britain.'

He taps the table with his finger, like he's pressing some sort of button that sends stupid rules up to God for approval. He seems strangely liberated, though, and leans back in his chair, confident I will ask him many questions about his new and wise dictat.

'Because if it were me,' I say, 'and I realised I was walking at the exact same pace as someone else, I would probably check my phone or slow down or something. But on the other hand, if someone else does it *to* me, I will *not* slow down, because that's playing right into their hands, you know, and I have my pride.'

A waiter wanders by and I ask him for tea. Colin nods to himself for a second and I allow him this, because he's clearly weighing up the pros and cons of my statement.

'Like, you turn up to the pub to wish Pete a happy birthday,' he says. 'And you're the only bloke who's brought something. Everyone else is like, "Happy birthday, I'll get you a pint." And you turn up with a Superdrug bag with a new shaving kit inside and everyone looks at you like you're obsessed with him or something. *And* you're expected to get him a pint on top of that. That's the real kicker. The pint on top.'

I nod my silent understanding and glance outside at the high street. That bloke who's always in Greggs is in Greggs again. By the window, I notice all the people walking by. I notice, too, that they are all managing to walk in very different areas of the pavement *and* at varying degrees of pace. They're nailing it. It's terrific to watch.

'You never see it happening to other people,' I say. 'Maybe because there's no way of knowing. They blend in, the people who do it, but they walk among us. I suppose you just assume that the pace-jacker and their victim are a couple and it's that very assumption I object to the most.'

Colin points at me. 'It's like the assumption that if you've bought someone a present you should also get them a pint.'

'Yes!' I say, jumping on this, because incredibly it's the first time he's addressed my important problem. 'Yes it *is* a bit like that.'

And then a memory slides by. A pub. A birthday. Pete.

'Wait. Pete's birthday was ages ago,' I say.

'Hmm?'

'Why are you talking about Pete's birthday? I was there. You didn't get him a shaving kit.'

'What did *you* get him?'

'A pint. Why are you telling me all this now?'

'We're not far off your birthday. I'm just preparing you. Managing your expectations. Join me in experimenting with perverting the rules of so-called "society". Don't expect a gift, yeah?'

'It's kind of you to include me in this experiment.'

He smiles to himself, like he's played a blinder. He must feel like a hundred bucks.

'Anyway,' he says. 'What do *you* want to talk about?'

Ice Dungeon!

The ice dungeon is very old,
You can smell the age,
You can feel the cold.
The forbidding echoes,
The hollow silence!
Everything is imprisoned,
In this place of violence!

I have a terrible sense of foreboding as I drive home, which I hope the evocative poem above has put you in the mood for.

My wife has sent me a text, gleefully informing me that she has been going through some old boxes…and found a purple notebook.

'My past has caught up with me,' I'd immediately thought. 'And now I must prepare.'

I'd assumed that this notebook was perhaps lost in the mists of time. I hadn't seen it in years, but for a while, in the late 1980s, the purple notebook and me were inseparable.

'Maybe she's not opened it,' I think. 'Maybe she's just decided to tell me about a purple notebook she found.' But I decide that if she hadn't opened it, she probably wouldn't have texted, otherwise she'd just be texting me random boring moments in her life, like 'Just popping upstairs' or 'Sneeze!'

I decide I am going to have to face the truth: my wife has found a series of pompous poems I wrote when I was eleven years old.

Poems. Poems that deal with Issues. Poems that offer solutions. Poems written in Loughborough in 1988, where it was all kicking off. Poems like 'Ice Dungeon!', 'Bluebells' and – as if any of us could forget – 'Race'.

I park the car and traipse up the few stairs to my front door, ready to face my fate. I don't even have to get my keys out. It swings open and there's my wife, looking delighted.

'"The damp bars!"' she shouts. '"The confined cage!"'

'Ice Dungeon!' She is quoting from 'Ice Dungeon!'

'"The rotten walls are in a state of rage!"'

'Hello…' I say, hoping to distract her from any talk of furious walls. 'How was—'

'"The solitary portcullis stays in its place!"' she yells, closing the door behind me and bringing out the book for 'Ice Dungeon!'s powerful conclusion. '"Until you meet the gloomy dungeon…*face to face*."'

She closes her eyes and allows us a moment of contemplative silence, which I hadn't put at the end of the poem, but which had always been my hope might happen naturally anyway.

I realise none of this is good news. For a start, 'Ice Dungeon!' doesn't seem to have provoked any of the questions inside her that I'd intended for the reader. She is not questioning the nature of the justice system, nor cottoned on to the use of ice as a metaphor for evolving generational attitudes. Instead, she's followed me into the kitchen and has moved on to 'Bluebells'.

'"A blue shade of mist! All across the landscape! That world you enter! The earth you escape!"'

'You're exclaiming too much,' I say, flicking on the kettle and shaking my head. '"Bluebells" has no exclamation marks. It was my intention to—'

But she doesn't want to listen. I am amazed. She has the poet, right here in her house, yet is wasting any opportunity to learn from him! I despair on behalf of my fellow poets, if this is the attitude modern audiences take.

She finishes with a flourish…

'"You take your camera, your rations as well…you sit on the grass, near a bluebell."'

'That was better, you did a lot less exclaiming,' I say, but she's already hungrily trying to find her next poem. I suppose it is good that I have awakened her love for poetry, but equally, this is not good news for a number of reasons. The main one is I now know she's going to spend the afternoon following me around the house reading at me and laughing.

Still. Was Shakespeare appreciated in his day? Did the twentieth century truly value T.S. Eliot? Yes, on both counts.

I suppose there comes a time in every man's life where something in our past catches up with us, exposing for just a moment who we were and asking us to deal with it. Perhaps the choices we make today will be the things we hope we won't be faced with tomorrow. Maybe I will write a poem about this.

'"Race!"' she shouts, as I close the door to my study, leaving her standing in the hallway. '"Is it just about your face?"'

Or maybe I won't.

The Craving

I am driving home with a huge multipack of Ferrero Rocher sitting in a plastic bag beside me.

'What a good husband I am,' I think, modestly, 'buying my wife a huge multipack of Ferrero Rocher.'

I glance at it. There are forty-eight individually wrapped Ferrero Rocher within its plastic casing, I notice. I suddenly feel that there is something about the vast quantity of Ferrero Rocher sitting inside that somehow takes away from the romance of my gesture. It is essentially a catering pack of Ferrero Rocher, and it is hard to be romantic with a catering pack of *anything*.

'Oh well,' I think. 'In a day or two, all these Ferrero Rocher will be gone, and I can go back to buying those three-packs you get in garages, just like the ambassador probably does, now there's a recession on.'

My wife has decided that even though it is some months now since she gave birth to our son, she still gets cravings. Unusually, these cravings tend not to be for beetroot or cabbage or yams, but for Ferrero Rocher and bacon double cheeseburgers.

I've decided not to mention anything, as she has read a lot more books about these things than I have, and also, I seem to be having sympathy cravings for bacon double cheeseburgers. I suppose this means I am very sensitive, in addition to being the good husband I mentioned earlier, and which you agreed with.

At home, I reveal the catering pack of Ferrero Rocher.

'That is *brilliant*!' she says, delighted, pawing at them. 'I've been *craving* one of those!'

The next day, I am in the kitchen listening to the radio, when I pass the magnificent plastic box of chocolates.

'That's strange,' I think. 'She's hardly touched them.'

There is just one empty space, next to row upon row of crinkly golden balls.

'She must've just had the one,' I think. 'And then thought, "Well, that's enough for me."'

I start to wonder if she is ill.

The next day, I glance again at the box. One more has gone. But only one. That's just two gone. And forty-six remaining. Perhaps her cravings are subsiding, I think. But probably, she is very ill.

It is a similar story the next day. Three gone, forty-five remaining. Unusually slow progress.

But the *next*…the Ferrero Rochers remain *untouched*.

I am confused. Perhaps I have misjudged the situation. Perhaps our sleep deprivation has finally claimed another two parents. Or perhaps she is eating these out of politeness. Perhaps she never even *liked* Ferrero Rocher, and then I come home and arrogantly present her with a year's supply, unreasonably expecting her to munch her way through them in a heartbeat.

I am a bad husband, I now realise, putting this kind of chocolate-based pressure on my small wife. Do I not understand the woman I married at all?

To make her feel better, I make a cup of tea and carefully place a Ferrero Rocher on a small white plate, like aristocrats do, and take it to the living room, where I slowly eat it while watching *Countdown*. This is a selfless act which states in no uncertain terms: 'We are in this together!'

I am startled, then, a day later, when I pass the box again and do a quick head count. Because there are forty-five remaining.

'But I ate one,' I think. 'I definitely ate one. It was a selfless gesture. It was supposed to say, "We are in this together!"'

And then I realise something with horror.

Slowly, I walk to the kitchen bin and peer inside.

There are Ferrero Rocher wrappings everywhere, mixed in with the cracked eggshells and old pasta.

Okay, there are not that *many* Ferrero Rocher wrappings, but there are enough. Enough to tell me what's been going on.

My wife has been *secretly replacing* Ferrero Rochers in the Ferrero Rocher box so it looks like she hasn't been eating lots of Ferrero Rocher! This is the type of behaviour an addict displays! Secretive! Shameful! Hiding the evidence! Keeping a stash! Masking their actions! Wearing one face in public, but underneath, at home…a shivering, juddery mess with a fearful, uncontrollable habit. She is addicted!

I instantly know what to do.

I open the door to the garden then wrap a small pebble in a Ferrero Rocher wrapper. I hide it three rows down. When she gets to this one, she will know I know. And I will know she knows I know.

But how *fast* will this happen? How bad is this addiction?

The next morning, as I sip my tea by the window, my wife walks into the room, and looks at me, ashamed.

Material

I am in the middle of town, waiting to meet Colin for a quick bite to eat.

I am eager to see him. Since he moved into his nursery, I have seen him less and less. I like to imagine he is spending a lot more time sitting cross-legged on the floor, playing with bricks.

We are planning on hitting Chinatown, and then, who knows? Cinema? Bowling? Another Chinese? The world is our oyster sauce.

But when he arrives, he looks grumpy.

'What's wrong?' I say.

'Nothing,' he mumbles.

In the Chinese restaurant, I wait for him to tell me that chopsticks would be better if they had a small coiled spring between them, as he always tells me when we're in a Chinese restaurant. He does not do this, however, even when I make quite a show of holding mine up and clicking them together. He simply remains quiet and pale.

'So what've you been up to?' I ask, and I can't wait for the answer. His latest plan to bag a woman, perhaps. Or an exciting idea for a terrific new business model!

'Not much,' he says, sniffily, and stares out of the window at a man carrying a box of fruit.

Something is wrong with Colin. I begin to worry that the strength of our friendship has been eroded somewhat by him moving into his nursery. Or…what if he's met someone else? No, I tell myself. He's probably just feeling down. He might have light carbon monoxide poisoning from the new flat. I have learned it is always better to remain positive like this.

So I decide to cheer him up.

I tell him I recently thought I'd accidentally ordered a prostitute as a birthday present for my wife.

He raises his eyebrows, and nods, bored, then shovels some more Kung Pao chicken in his mouth.

I need to try something else.

'I pretended my name was Alfonso in a foreign Starbucks and then lost my nerve when they shouted "Alfonso!"' I say, looking for any sort of reaction, but losing confidence, and almost saying it apologetically.

But it's no good.

'Look…there's something I want to tell you,' he says. 'But I'm afraid you'll use it.'

'Use it?'

'Use it. You'll use it. There is no way you won't use it.'

'I won't use it.'

'Trust me, you will use it. There are some things I think you'll use, like the girl I chatted up on the bus in two minutes flat, and some things I know you *won't*, like me living in a nursery.'

'I used that nursery thing quite a lot,' I say. 'It's how your mum found out you were living in a nursery, if you remember.'

'And the girl? The girl on the bus?'

There is no way I'm using that, but I do a sort of half-nod, half-shake, which he seems to be satisfied with.

'You know, all this throws up an interesting philosophical point about the nature of our friendship,' says Colin, wisely. 'It throws up all sorts of questions about society, too. What we mean to each other. How our stories and experiences are shared and traded. Whether our standing is affected by those experiences. Whether you and I – and indeed friends everywhere – are somehow forever bonded by an as-yet unwritten contract of communal storytelling.'

Well, he didn't actually say all that. He said, 'All this throws up an interesting philosophical point about the nature of friendship,' and then when I said 'what is it?' he just looked blank and stuck his bottom lip out.

But keen to see my friend coming back to life, and excited by the prospect of his story, I urge him to tell me.

He does. I am amazed and delighted by it.

He puts his fingers to his lips, and says 'Ssssh' and winks. I nod. And then he sees what is still in his hand.

'You know,' he says, pointing with the chopstick. 'These'd be a lot better with a spring in the middle.'

I go home happy, my promise to keep Colin's story to myself totally intact.

Once there, I immediately tell my wife, so I might as well tell you.

Colin, while working, had been introduced to a little old lady, who had looked him up and down, taking him in, and not seeming immediately to approve.

'Can you turn the lights up, please?' she'd said, indicating the room. 'I'm deaf!'

'Ha ha ha ha ha ha!' replied Colin, loudly, to show appreciation for her joke and, he hoped, for the elderly in general. 'Ha ha ha ha ha!'

She stared at him.

'What are you laughing at?' she'd said, grumpily. 'Are you laughing at me?'

'What? No!' said Colin.

'Because you seem to be laughing at me,' she said.

Colin chuckled, but it was a nervous chuckle, a chuckle that implied he hoped the end of this conversation was near. But still she stared at him.

'No, you see, you asked me to turn the *lights* up,' said Colin, 'and then said it was because you're *deaf*!'

'Yes,' she said, firmly. 'I need you to turn the lights up because I am deaf and I need to *lip read*.'

Colin stared at her, trying to work out if she was joking.

'I really don't see why you found that peculiar,' she said, shaking her head and looking away.

Colin quietly turned up the lights.

I finish telling my wife this story with a little flourish. I use our living room dimmer switch to great comic effect.

'And why did he not want you to use that?' she asks.

'I think he thought this particular interaction made him look silly. I mean, he also doesn't like how I keep telling people he is living in a nursery he accidentally moved into, even though he is living in a nursery he accidentally moved into.'

'Well, I bet you were scared,' she says, nodding to herself, like she has already decided.

I make a purposefully confused face, but she ignores it, so I make it even more purposeful and confused.

'Scared,' she explains, mysteriously, 'because Colin has power over you.'

She points at me.

'He is your *muse*,' she says, and walks away.

I stand, blinking and alone, in the living room, and think about what she's said. Could Colin be my muse? I suppose I do tell people about him a lot. But no. He is not my muse. He is my friend. My friend who lives in a nursery. And if he *were* my muse, how did this happen? I mean, Jagger had Marianne Faithfull. Dylan had Edie Sedgwick. Billy Joel had Christine Brinkley, and Picasso had Dora Maar.

I've got a thirty-three-year-old man who lives in a nursery.

'I need to get a better muse,' I panic. 'What if Colin had been Picasso's muse? There's no *way* Colin would've let him experiment with cubism! Colin would've said it was mental and told him to draw properly or not at all! With Colin as my muse, I dare say I will *never* be as good at painting or art as Picasso!'

It is then that I hear my wife, clattering about in the kitchen.

I walk towards her, distractedly, and stand in the doorway, and watch as she lovingly tends to our son. She hums along to the radio, and I imagine how comforting that must be for him, to be so surrounded by her. And I watch her as she washes the vegetables – some home-grown – that in a moment she'll boil and then purée with home-made stock that she spends hour upon hour making so that he'll grow up big and strong and healthy. And I watch as she leans over him, and feeds him, nurtures him, strokes his hair, *loves* him.

'Hmm,' I think, my hand on my chin, taking in this scene of warmth and family. 'So I wonder what Colin's up to.'

I get my phone out and text him.

'Just tripped up in the street, *totally* distracted by a hottie!' he replies.

I nod.

I can use that.

Emergency

There is a medical emergency at home!

A medical emergency!

I feel pompous and important as I tut at the traffic all around me, getting in my way with their trivial, less important business.

'There is a medical emergency!' I want to shout from the window of my car. 'Move along now! You can undertake your trivial and less important business when I pass!'

I switch the radio from Magic to Radio 4 to fully capture the mood of the situation.

'I wish I could swear at strangers at times like that,' I think to myself, all maudlin. 'It would be so un-British to let loose and start shouting "flick you!" or "flick off!" at people.'

I promise myself that before I hit fifty I will do it – though for now there is a medical emergency to concentrate on.

But as I get maybe a mile or two from home, I start to feel strange myself. I open the windows as I break into an odd sweat, and have to turn the radio back to Magic for comfort.

Inside the house, I find my wife slumped on the sofa, clinging weakly to a mug of tea, our baby son asleep upstairs.

'To bed with you!' I order, and I feel great because I am a man taking charge of a situation. I will have to remember to tell the neighbours about the time I saved the day!

'But…' she tries.

'No buts! I will feed the boy when he wakes. Off to bed!'

She nods, bleary-eyed, and starts to trudge up the stairs,

and now I slump onto the sofa myself, thinking maybe I can score a quick nap or something.

But then…a noise like I have never heard before.

I leap up the stairs – and stop in my tracks.

Now, I have seen my wife be sick before. I have held her hair back over sinks and toilets. I have held and stroked her hand as she's sat on the floor, cross-legged, drunk and crying, with that evening's cocktails and canapés smeared all the way down her pretty new party dress. And there has always been something sweet about it. Something bonding.

But never, ever did I realise my tiny wife was capable of this.

I stand, open-mouthed and shocked, my eyebrows three feet above my head, as my wife spins from wall to wall, trying to steady herself, but each time being launched in the other direction by a powerful new jet of terrible. She is making the sound a waste disposal makes when everyone finally decides they might need to call the landlord.

I am at once appalled and inspired.

'Medical emergency!' I declare. 'Phone!'

I grab the phone as my wife continues her strange liquid ballet on the landing, every so often managing another step towards the bathroom, and I feel my own stomach tightening.

I dial one of the 118 numbers.

'Medical emergency!' I say. 'I need the number for NHS Direct or something!'

'Sorry?' says the lady.

'NHS Direct!' I say. 'Can I have the number for NHS Direct?'

My knees buckle a little and I can feel something rising in my throat.

'Chicken!' shouts my wife, who's finally in the bathroom. 'I think that chicken we had was bad yesterday!'

Food poisoning! We've got food poisoning!

'MHS?' says the lady on the phone.

'N…NHS,' I say. 'As in "the NHS". Quickly, please!'

In the other room, I hear my son jolt awake and immediately, piercingly start crying. I rush through, pick him up, try to comfort him.

'M for Mother?' says the lady.

'N! N for November! NHS Direct! We need to speak to a nurse!'

I carry my son out of his room and nearly slip on the landing, my foot now soggy and slapping the floor as I carry him to the bathroom where my wife is being *spectacularly* loud.

'I have the number,' says the lady, 'would you like me to put you through?'

'I should take this chance to swear at her,' I think to myself. 'I should say, "No! Don't put me flicking through! Let me pop off and buy a flicking pen from Ryman's so I can spend flicking ages writing it down!"' But I don't – I sigh and say, 'Yes please!'

My own sickness is starting to hit properly, perhaps accelerated by the noises from the bathroom, the soggy foot, the tiny baby screaming in my arms, and then the woman on the end of the phone, the woman who can hear the stress in my voice, the only other person in the world who can hear what's going on in this house, this flicking woman says…'Have a *great* evening!'

I pause to take in the scene around me.

And then I, Danny Wallace, finally go flicking ape-spit.

The Hug

I have received an email from an old school friend inviting me to meet up and asking if he can suggest a date.

'Yes!' I write back. 'That would be lovely!'

He does.

We meet up a week later at a restaurant down a side street in South London. When I arrive, he is smartly dressed and handsome and grins widely. I go for the handshake, but he's already started the hug and so I join in slightly late, which is awkward.

'I must remember to hug him first when the night is over,' I think to myself. 'I must not join in late this time.'

The restaurant is snug and quiet. There are two other men in a corner, staring intently into each other's eyes, and the place is very dimly lit. I sit down on my chair, but it is not very comfortable. It's too high, the table's too low, and I'm forced to lean right the way forward. My friend does the same, and smiles.

A waiter skips over and places a small candle right between us.

Now we are two men in a dimly lit restaurant inches from each other's faces, our hands almost touching, lit only by flickering candlelight.

'Well, this is unusual,' I think.

We order some rosé because it's nearly summer.

'So what's going on?' I say, as the drinks arrive. 'Are you married? Got kids?'

He laughs. Quite a high laugh, and then he shakes his head dramatically.

'No!' he says. 'Not really in the market for that!'

'Ha ha!' I say. 'Fair enough!'

'Actually, I'm newly single,' he says, and he looks a little sad. I make a sad face too.

'Never mind!' he says, suddenly brightening. 'I'm here now!'

'Yes, you are!' I say, and we clink our rosé together.

I cast my eyes around the room. Another two men have arrived. I realise they are drinking rosé too. I notice the music. I think it's Kenny G.

And then I realise I'm in a South London gay hotspot.

'It's good to see you,' says my friend, and there's a momentary pause, and I smile, but it's a *weird* smile, because I'm remembering his email.

'Suggest a date,' I think. 'He said suggest a *date*. What if by "date"…'

'So how about you?' he says. 'Married?'

Oh. What do I say here? What if I sound like I'm making it up, as if I've agreed to a date but don't fancy him? He's on the rebound! He's fragile! It would be terrible if he thought I didn't fancy him! Or what if when I say I'm married, it sounds somehow homophobic? Not that it ordinarily could or would, but what if I say it wrong? What if I say it in a way that implies it is correct to be married? I am absolutely terrified of sounding homophobic! I even have a special face I make when someone tells me they're gay. A face that says, 'Really? That's terrific! Come round! Use my bed!'

'I'm…you know,' I say, nodding for no apparent reason, and then I think *grow up*. 'I'm married to a wife.'

I'm married to a wife?

'*My* wife, I mean,' I say, but that's *obvious*, and now I sound like a man pretending he's married to a wife, or worse – I sound like I'd prefer to deny her very existence! Who goes to a gay restaurant to meet a gay man and drink rosé and listen to Kenny G while pretending his wife doesn't exist? A man at a crossroads about to come out, that's who!

My friend nods at me. He seems slightly concerned. Perhaps he's seen this before. Perhaps he always had his suspicions about me. Perhaps he's worried I've misunderstood the word 'date'. Perhaps he's wondering how he can let me down gently.

'That's good,' he says, encouragingly, as if it's important I deal with this head on. 'I'd heard you were married.'

'Yes,' I say, and then, inexplicably, 'To a little *lady*, though.'

Great. Now I'm coming across as gay, homophobic *and* a little sexist. I wanted to make the right impression. Instead, I'm a Nazi.

It gets to dessert. He orders one. The waiter asks if *I'd* like a spoon as well. I say yes, just to show how cool I am with whatever sexuality I currently seem to be. Even *I'm* confused.

As we leave, I remember to hug first, but he's gone for the handshake. I ignore this, and just hold him for a second, tight.

'I'll be back in London soon,' he says, looking a little uncomfortable.

'It's a date,' I say.

The Hen Party

My friend Rich is about to meet my parents for the first time, and I've instructed him to be on his best behaviour. 'No rude words,' I tell him. 'Not even ones that you claim afterwards are okay because they're in the medical dictionary.'

He nods.

'And no talking about women!'

'I will be fine,' he says. 'Look into my eyes.'

I look into his eyes. I remain unconvinced.

'Medical dictionary words still count,' I say, my finger in the air.

We join my parents in a quiet little pub, and Rich begins his Saturday afternoon charm offensive. He is witty, and urbane, and my parents seem to think he is a delight. He regales them with stories of nobility and intrigue, but I am nervous, knowing that at any moment we might have to get a medical dictionary out.

Moments later, there is noise from somewhere in the corner. A large group of girls has arrived with bottles of wine and excited chatter. I catch a glimpse of a pink feather boa. It's a hen party.

Rich, to his credit, only stares at each of them individually for a second or two, before doing it once again, and then continuing with his story. This is almost unheard of.

'Good, Rich,' I think. 'There will be time to stare at women later.'

But then, suddenly, one of the girls is standing at our table.

'Excuse me,' she says, looking at my dad. 'I'm getting married soon, and my friends have given me this game I have to play today.'

I start to sweat, slightly.

'I have to do what it says on these cards…'

Oh, no. This is going to be bawdy in some way. And in front of my parents!

'I have to give a stranger an erotic massage…'

The words hang in the air.

'Oh,' says my dad, embarrassed.

'Oh,' says my mum, trying to pretend she's not.

'Oh God,' I think. 'No!' I can't have an erotic massage in a pub! And nor can my dad! We can't have one *anywhere*!

I blink a couple of times, and then look to Rich. He is remaining silent. This is not like Rich at all. He is behaving. Behaving, because I *told* him to.

'Him!' I nearly yell. '*He'll* do it!'

Rich breaks into a wide smile.

'Well, you *are* getting married,' he says, and she smiles too, and then begins to massage his shoulders, erotically, inches away from my parents' faces.

'You're very good at massaging!' says my mum, kindly. 'Are you a masseuse?'

'No,' says the girl, continuing.

We sit in awkward silence for a bit. I sip at my drink.

'There you go!' she says, after maybe twelve or thirteen hours, and Rich says thanks, and the girls all start applauding. He waves, and then brilliantly returns to the conversation. I am proud of my friend.

But then, one minute later, she's back.

'I'm so sorry, but you're the only men in the pub…I have to do this next one…'

She shows us the card. It is what you might call a little

graphic, involving zippers and kneeling. She looks again at my dad.

'He'll do it!' I shout, pointing at Rich. '*He* will!'

Rich rolls his eyes at me and casts a glance to my parents, as if I am *always* forcing him to engage in lewd acts in the middle of the day.

'Okay...' he sighs, heavily, before standing up. The girls start to whoop.

'Goodness,' says my mum. 'You all seem to be having a lot of fun!'

'Mum,' I say, trying to distract her. 'How are you...enjoying...life?'

It is an awful conversational gambit, but she and my father look me straight in the eye and begin to tell me how they're enjoying life. I listen intently, or pretend to, because all I can think about is the fact that my friend is engaging in a pretend obscene act with a total stranger on the other side of the table.

It takes forever. And then Rich sits back down and continues to chat as if nothing has happened. My parents look a little traumatised.

'Well,' he says, a little later, as we leave the pub. 'I think that went very well.'

'You engaged in lewd acts with strangers!' I say. 'There was kneeling and very little in the way of explanation!'

'*You* made me do it!' he says, offended. 'And anyway, how would I have explained it?'

'You could've just...I dunno...'

'I *could've* explained it,' he says, grumpily. 'But I would've needed a medical dictionary.'

The Flasher

I am in the lounge of a major airline and all is well.

There is a happy-faced, whistling woman, wandering around handing out free fried chicken. A friendly concierge is sidling up to people, shaking their hands and making small talk and offering them wine. There are dozens of pensioners, sitting silently and staring soulfully into the middle distance.

And now a lady has walked in wearing a fantastic hat.

I say 'fantastic hat' as if I'm expecting you to visualise exactly how fantastic this hat is, but believe me – it's fantastic. The only way I can possibly describe it is to call it a Bollywood Sombrero.

It is burgundy, I think, with a wide rim, and big gold leaves, and small mirrors hanging from the underside that glint and wink and sparkle like things I'm sure I've seen draped from the necks of Bollywood dancers.

'I need to tell someone about this fantastic hat,' I think to myself, and immediately reach for my phone.

But it is getting late where I am, and much later still back home, and I am worried about waking someone just to tell them about a fantastic hat.

So I decide to tweet it. Seeing a hat is just the type of quality observation the people following me on Twitter want to hear about, I confidently decide.

'I am in an airport lounge,' I type. 'A woman has walked in with an extraordinary hat. It's like a Bollywood Sombrero.'

There. It's off my chest. I no longer have to look at the woman with the fantastic hat, and can instead concentrate on the free wine. I take some fried chicken from the whistling lady and sit back.

And then I check my responses.

'I want a picture!' says one person.

'Can you take a picture?' says another.

Uh-oh. I can see what's happening. My tweet was simply *too* exciting. I should have known news of a fantastic hat several thousand miles away would catch fire like this. I just hope the press don't get wind.

'I'll try and work out a way…' I bluff, hoping this will be enough to stave off the rampant enthusiasm for a Bollywood Sombrero, but apparently it is not.

'Take a secret picture,' offers one respondent, immediately. 'Pretend you are sending a text!'

'You can do it if you pretend to be reading something on your phone,' says another. 'Make sure you move your eyes left to right while you press the camera button!'

I break into a small sweat. I don't want to do this. I don't want to take a picture of this woman and her fantastic hat. I'll look odd! And yet I can already feel I am being forced into it by this group of hat-obsessed strangers.

I look up, and see that the woman has now hung her fantastic hat over her suitcase. It tempts me, like a lovely sunflower. I look again at the responses. More have come in, making their unreasonable hat-based demands of me.

'Why did I tell people of this fantastic hat?' I think to myself, shaking my head, sadly. 'I bet this is just what happened to Joseph and his Dreamcoat, although that's something I'd have to check.'

So then, beaten down, and when no one is looking, I raise my phone, switch it to camera, pretend I'm sending a text, use the zoom function…and snap a picture.

It is rubbish. It is dark, and blurry, and in no way looks like a fantastic hat.

Immediately, I know I'm going to have to get closer. But I have learnt a lesson already. The camera made its camera noise. If I'd been closer, I'd have been rumbled, but no one heard. I switch the camera to silent. I feel like I'm in *The Cube* and have just used up my Trial Run.

I get up, casually, and wander over to the fantastic hat. As I get closer, I pretend I've just had a text, and now I'm just nine or ten feet away from the woman, and I pause, and stand there and make my eyes go from left to right, and now I *know* I can do it, now I know this can *work*, so I press the camera option, and I choose my moment, and I hit the button, and…

People all around look up at me. A man puts down his paper.

The flash went off. I was *quite obviously* taking a picture of a fantastic hat.

When I sit down, I check my tweets.

'Remember to turn off the automatic flash,' says one, but I don't really take it in, as I'm drinking a *lot* of wine.

Virus

I have arrived at my destination: a tiny, stinking hotel room next to a motorway somewhere two hours north of Tokyo. I am excited. I have two days to explore! Some people simply stay in their hotel rooms watching foreign versions of *Strictly Come Dancing* and wondering why they chose *that* host to replace Bruce Forsyth.

Not me! I have just forty-eight hours to explore the *whole* of Japan. Japan! Home of robots! Japan! Ninjas and samurai skipping hand-in-hand! Japan! They sell noodles! JAPAN!

Hang on…

A grubby slip of paper slides under my door. It reads thusly:

'Dear guest,
 We take precaution to treat you with accommodation of highest hygiene standards.'

I look around my small room and take in the handprint above the bed, the mould blushing the walls, and the improbably long hair artfully draped across the back of the sticky door, making it look like the Thames at the start of *EastEnders*. But who cares? I'm in *Japan*! I go back to the letter.

'Infectious gastroenteritis caused by novo virus is common occurrence in this period of the year. By any chance, if you happened to vomit in your room, we kindly request you to contact the Front Desk, and we will take care to clean it up. Thanks you, the General Manager.'

I blink once or twice, and then read it again.

I have not vomited in my room. I am *sure* of it. Why did they think I had vomited in my room? Why were they *worried* I would vomit in my room? Did I look like the sort of person who books a room in a hotel and then vomits in it? Do people simply book rooms in Japan to vomit in? I'd come a long way, if they thought that was all I was after. I'd have used my own house, or simply visited a friend and vomited round theirs.

But I am worried now that someone else *might* have vomited in my room, and that their vomitous outburst was perhaps heard by the General Manager, and that the General Manager had taken his sweet time drafting some kind of letter to warn me – without actually warning me – that I am about to catch the novo virus. No! I want ninjas and noodles! Not the novo virus!

The novo virus sounds a little too much like the norovirus for my liking: the virus that the British media and furious, cross-eyed GPs told us was coming for us all before Christmas. I believed them. I believed them when they said that 100 million Britons would all be face down in the gutters, juddering about, that the economy would crash and that life as we know it would be changed forever. It would be the start of a global pandemic to rival anything the Bible could have thrown our way, and now, suddenly, this small slip of paper shoved under my door in a Japanese Travelodge seems proof that The End has Begun.

I instantly get on-line and check up on the novo virus.

'The virus is easily transmitted from one person to another. It can be transmitted by contact with an infected person; by consuming contaminated food or water, or by contact with contaminated surfaces or objects.'

My eyes flit to the half glass of tap water that sits on the dusty table in front of me. I break into a sweat. I read on.

'An early sign of infection is excessive sweating.'

I begin to sweat *excessively*.

I calm myself and hatch a plan. I will simply, throughout my short and exciting stay in Japan, avoid contact with people, eat no food and drink no water, and refuse to touch any surface or object whatsoever. I feel pleased with myself for preparing in this way.

And then I stand in my room and sway for a bit. This isn't so bad. This is, after all, still technically *Japan*.

And then I realise I am being silly. I am British. I am supposed to stand tall in the face of adversity. We are a nation of explorers. Of adventurers. And I am a man. A *grown* man. This alone surely makes me immune to the novo virus.

I decide to go outside. I will be brave. And also, at least no one will ever have vomited outside.

Downstairs at reception, an elderly lady behind the counter smiles at me. At least, I *think* she smiles at me. I can't see, because she's wearing a surgical mask over her mouth. 'Don't panic,' I think. 'Plenty of people in Japan wear surgical masks around their mouths. This hotel is not infected with the novo virus. This hotel is merely taking preventative measures. No one has vomited in my room.'

I take a deep breath and instantly regret it. What if I've just breathed in the novo virus? What if someone has just vomited in reception? That would explain the mask! I break into another sweat. Worrying about this new sweat causes a subsequent subset sweat. Soon, I am sure I will dissolve. Did the internet say anything about dissolving? Was dissolving a sign of the novo virus?

Panicked, I head for the door.

Through the window, I spot someone else hurrying along. She is wearing a surgical mask, just like the lady behind reception. 'The fumes,' I think, reassuringly. 'She is merely avoiding the fumes of the automobiles. That lady is very unlikely to have vomited in my room. This must not spoil my enjoyment of Japan.'

I walk outside and pass the woman. She looks sweaty. Not excessively sweaty, but sweaty enough. I hold my breath as she hurries by. My eyes are wide with paranoia. But I must do this. I am British!

The Japanese version of *Strictly Come Dancing* is called *Shall We Dance?* I stare at it for an hour, wondering why they chose *that* host to represent Bruce Forsyth.

I look at my half glass of water, longingly.

Emergency Two

There is a plumbing emergency!

A *plumbing emergency*!

'We should phone Mr Barker,' says my wife.

I haven't been back long, but I'm thinking very clearly.

'I don't want to phone Mr Barker,' I say. 'Mr Barker always makes me call him Mr Barker. It makes me uncomfortable, this need of his to emasculate me. Whenever he does any work for us I have to resist the urge to genuflect and bow. He makes me feel like an infant, with all this "Mr Barker" nonsense.'

We stand for a moment and stare at the inch-deep water that's taken over our basement. It seems to be getting worse.

'Maybe we should phone Mr Barker,' I say.

But my wife finds another solution. A local firm of plumbers who promise to be round in an instant.

An instant later, the doorbell rings.

'I'm Geoff,' says Geoff, and I'm delighted. 'Are you Mr Wallace?'

At last! I am the Mister in this tradesman trade-off.

'Come in, *Geoff*!' I say, proudly. 'Come in and see our basement!'

We have had to agree to pay Geoff ninety-four pounds to come round and lend us his expertise.

'Well, you've got some kind of leak,' he says, and immediately I know this is ninety-four pounds well spent. 'It's not the washing machine, but the water must be coming in from somewhere. Did it rain last night?'

I say that I think it did.

'Probably the excess water from the rain,' he says.

It's about now that I realise I could probably be a plumber.

Geoff and myself inspect the basement before he decides to take a look at the outside, and – bingo!

'There were some leaves in the drain,' he laughs. 'I've removed them. That should sort it.'

I am ashamed that I did not think to look for leaves in the drain. It turns out that ninety-four pounds is a small price to pay to get him out of my house and end my embarrassment, for I have failed as a man. I mop up the water as he leaves, quietly, and it feels like I am mopping up my dreams.

But the next day, the water is back, and deeper than ever.

'There are no leaves in the drain!' I say, on the phone, confused.

'We'll send someone round!' says the plumbing firm, but I wonder what they could possibly do this time. I become paranoid I am going to be ripped off for another ninety-four pounds.

I know exactly what I need. I need a wingman. I need to up the level of testosterone in the house. They won't dare just blame leaves with two men in the house!

Colin knocks at the door. He seems happy. He had a date last night.

'We went back to mine and watched *Death Wish 3* on telly. I was enjoying telling her which bits were filmed in America and which bits were filmed in England.'

'It sounds like a magical evening,' I say, and he nods, misty-eyed. 'She probably thought you were about to propose.'

'So what's going on?'

'There's a leak in the basement but no one knows where it's coming from,' I say.

'Washing machine,' he says, flatly, and I hope he is not right, but know it will probably turn out that he is.

Ten minutes later, a new plumber is at our door, and I lead him down to the basement, while Colin puts on an I-know-all-about-drainage face.

'Well,' says this new one, John, after a bit. 'The question is, where is it coming from?'

He has certainly identified the question.

'You could do a dye test. Or we could get a small camera out, and check the drains outside for leaks.'

This all sounds quite expensive.

'You should probably get all this damp-proofed, too, just to be safe,' he adds, slapping a wall. 'We can do that sort of thing for you.'

Throughout, I have been nodding and uh-huh'ing and slapping the wall too, while my wingman has been humming and studying the back of a Jason Statham DVD cover he found.

'Okay, thanks John,' I say, trying to be manly, as I close the door.

It's only when he leaves that I realise – he hasn't actually done anything. I have just agreed to pay a man another ninety-four pounds to come round and simply describe our problem to us out loud. I've been doing that all morning for *free*.

'Where were *you*?' I say, turning to Colin, annoyed. 'Where was my wingman?'

'I'm telling you,' says Colin. 'Washing machine.'

In the end we call Mr Barker. It's the washing machine. I feel more like an infant than ever.

Colin asks me for ninety-four pounds.

The Toilet

The noises coming from the cubicle behind me are like nothing I've ever heard before.

They are terrifying.

I stand at the urinal, inches from the wall, staring straight in front of me in horror.

These noises are almost indescribable in their monstrousness. Almost, but not quite. They're low, and guttural, and random in their explosions and fizzes and pops. There is no way a normal human male can make this kind of sound. Not without thinking, 'There is no way I can be a normal human male.'

A short period of silence follows. I attempt to begin my own important business, but it is no good, because then – *boom* – the sound continues.

'Why is he doing this?' I think. 'Surely he *knows* someone else is in here? Who can do something like this with such casual abandon? Does he not know the rules? Has he no shame?'

And then I realise. He can't have heard me come in here. He thinks he's alone. A wave of guilt hits me. This poor man. This poor, strangely productive man. I should have made more noise. This is my fault. Maybe it is *I* who needs to relearn the rules. I'd been stealthy upon entry to the bathroom when in fact I should have coughed, or cleared my throat, or walked with heavier feet, alerting any hidden men of my presence.

Another awful noise slaps the silence and I snap out of my guilt. I need to let him know I'm in here. Stop this brazen madness. But I need to be careful. When he realises he's not been alone, he'll feel terrible. Self-conscious. Ashamed. I consider my next move. A cough? A cough would sound too obvious and make him wonder why I hadn't coughed earlier. So, being very careful and holding my trousers together at the top, I quietly creep towards the door, and then loudly open it, making heavy footsteps as I tramp back towards the urinal.

It works.

Everything has gone quiet, save for the quiet rustle of a newspaper behind a locked cubicle door, possibly the man's way of saying, 'Hi! There's someone in here!'

I smile. Normality has been restored. I attempt to begin once again my important business.

How strange, I think, that we have these little psychological tricks; these small unspoken behavioural nuances that allow society to function with a little less friction, and how nice that…

Boom.

My eyes widen. There are a couple of smaller booms.

He knows I'm in here! He *knows* and yet still he persists!

'Who would *do* something like this?' I think. 'Especially when I've gone to such extraordinary efforts to give him a second chance! Why is he punishing me this way?'

I realise I need to get out of here. I need to get my important business done. I begin.

And then – the most terrifying noise of all.

Is he… Please, no!

He's started to stand up. The newspaper is being put to one side.

I begin to panic. There is no way I can see this man. Not after what I've heard. Not after him hearing me hearing him! He knows I know, and I can't lock eyes with a man who knows I know!

There is something too disgraceful about the moment we've shared – too horrifying, too *personal*. Will we have to speak? Or will we just nod at one another, darkly, and with the dull and pained eyes of old soldiers wordlessly exchanging nods, knowing in their hearts they have seen *such things*?

I need to finish my important business, and quick – but then I hear him fastening his belt and I panic some more. He's clearing his throat, now, and then – the flush.

Quick! I think. Quick!

I manage to stop, and make my break for the sink, just as I hear the man turning the lock of his door. I begin to whistle, pointlessly, as if I've not got a care in the world and haven't just shared moments of incredible intimacy with a stranger in a toilet. Which is a sentence I never thought I'd write.

But I've acted *too* carefree, because I've spun the tap right round, and now there's water bouncing around the sink and lightly spraying my clothes.

I look down and see the front of my trousers has been badly affected.

'Whoops,' says the man.

We lock eyes in the mirror.

'*That's* embarrassing,' he says.

The Monkey

I am sitting quietly with Colin in the pub.

It is a far rarer thing than it used to be, finding me and Colin in the pub like this, but the baby is starting to sleep a little better these days, we're starting to get him into a routine, and means small slivers of normality are returning.

And then the text arrives.

'Oh, blimey,' I say, deflated. 'It's still going.'

'What?' says Colin, and I show him.

'Oh,' he says, understanding, and then taking a sip of his pint. 'You should really stop that.'

'I'm not doing it! It's being done! But not by me!'

'Still,' he says, stifling a burp. 'I think it compromises your artistic integrity. Makes me feel a bit dirty just sitting here with you.'

Colin is referring to a high-profile national advertising campaign I have recently become involved with.

In Egypt.

'It's not my fault!' I say, casting my eye around the pub for a sympathetic glance that never comes. 'I had literally nothing to do with it! Some Egyptian man did it!'

I read the text again.

'You're on a massive billboard in Cairo, hugging a monkey.'

I shake my head.

'Every week I get one of these. "You're hugging a monkey in Cairo. You're hugging a monkey in Luxor. Hey, you're hugging a monkey by the Suez."'

Colin shakes his head, and makes an understanding face.

'You hug *one* monkey, and you're tarred for life,' he says, sadly. 'In the North African region.'

Then he puts his pint down, like he's going to solve this.

'Talk me through how this happened.'

'Google,' I say. 'So I met a chimp one day and we got on and I had my picture taken with him. Stuck it on-line, used it as a profile pic. Next thing I know, some bloke working behind reception at the Africa Safari & Motel googles "funny monkey" or something, finds my picture, and launches a national advertising campaign. I'm all over Egypt.'*

'I suppose it's like when Tom Cruise advertises watches in Japan,' says Colin, confidently, and for a second this makes me feel better. But then I remember that Tom Cruise looks cool in his adverts, and I look like a man being touched by an ape.

'It's not *quite* the same,' I say, grabbing my phone. I text my friend back to ask where in Egypt he was. Moments later, I have my reply.

'Alexandria,' I say. 'Well, that's *all* I need. Now it's spread to Alexandria.'

'Is this a problem? How often are you in Alexandria?'

'I've never been, that's not the point. The point is, there are now billboards in Alexandria of me and a monkey.'

'You should get paid. You could make millions. You could tour Egypt. They'd be like, "Hey,, monkey man! You're the man who touches monkeys!"'

'Yeah, that'd be brilliant,' I say, quietly.

Actually, that *would* be brilliant.

'"Hey, monkey fiddler! Stop your chimp bothering!"'

'Look...'

'"Hey, Four-eyed Dr Dolittle! Please stop putting big pictures of your ape-liaisons all over our country! This is a place of magic and wonder! This is no place for comic bestiality!"'

---

* *fig 3, appendix*

I scowl at him and he stops.

'It's a strange career move, Dan, that's all I'm saying.'

'Colin, I don't know how to stop it. The campaign seems to have been a resounding success.'

'Does it?'

'It grows by the week.'

'Wow.'

'It's everywhere now. In Egypt, I mean.'

There is a moment of silence as Colin considers this.

'So it's pretty popular?'

'Seems to be.'

'And it's working?'

'Seems to be.'

'Well…then whatever my artistic reservations, I salute you. You have made your choices. You are a brave advertising pioneer, like Kerry Katona or Robert Webb, and it has paid off.'

'Really?'

He raises his glass.

'To the Africa Safari & Motel,' he says.

'To the Africa Safari & Motel,' I smile.

'And to Google,' he says. 'And to those who oppose the laws of copyright. And for anyone who's ever touched a monkey.'

I am just staring at him now.

'And to Kerry Katona.'

I put my pint down.

'*What*?' he says.

The Apocalypse

A few years ago, I was asked to present a TV show about the impending apocalypse, to which I cheerily agreed, because I think if there's going to be an apocalypse, it's important to make a light-hearted programme about it first.

'We need to film where there are people,' the director said to me, on the phone. 'People just going about their daily business, unaware…'

We meet at rush hour on Oxford Street and he has a surprise for me.

'We thought it might be good if you wore this…' he says.

It's a sandwich board. A sandwich board that reads, 'The End of the World is Nigh.'

'I will *do* this!' I say, importantly. 'It is for the good of the show!'

I strap myself in, knowing that while in some contexts this might make me look insane, with a television crew around me it will be clear why I am wearing it.

'So,' says the director. 'The opening…'

'Yes!' I say, and then I practise. *'THE END OF THE WORLD IS UPON US! According to the Bible, the last days –'*

'Great, great,' he says, and then he clasps his hands together. 'So I thought it'd be fun to see you, moving in among the crowd, walking and talking…'

'Absolutely.'

'And we would sort of crash zoom in and pick you out and then you'd start.'

'Sounds good.'

'So we'll get set up. When you see me wave, that's when you start.'

'Terrific. And where are you going to be?'

'We're going to be…' he points at quite an unusual spot behind him, '…just up there.'

'Oh,' I say. 'But that's…'

It's *miles* away. The director has pointed at the top floor of a building that might as well be in Germany. It's going to take him *ages* to get there and *ages* to set up. Which means that I'll be standing here, alone, in the middle of Oxford Street, wearing a huge 'The End of the World is Nigh' sign.

I start to feel a little uncomfortable.

The guys head off as I stand, more alone than I have ever been, a sign around my neck that quietly proclaims the end of the world, as strangers bump and jostle around me.

'Cheer up, might never happen,' sniggers one man, passing.

'TV show,' I try, pathetically, but even if people believe me, there are no cameras around, no runner with a clipboard, no evidence for my statement whatsoever, unless you look up at a very specific faraway building and are able to make out three tiny men who still weren't there yet. They're taking *forever*.

'Ha ha,' laughs someone else, and I try to smile at them, but that just makes me look madder, so I decide to fix my eyes on the building where what seems like hours later, I can finally see the crew.

'I'm very pleased you're there,' I whisper, into my microphone. 'I think people think I'm mad.'

And then I realise that now I look like I'm talking to myself.

So I keep quiet, but now some of the braver souls have started taking pictures of me on their mobile phones, one person even standing next to me with their thumbs up. But I can't say anything, can't explain myself, because I have to keep my eyes solely on the director, in case he waves, because if I miss that, we miss the shot…

So I just stare and stare, not moving, not blinking, while other people laugh or point at the weird, staring man of Oxford Street.

And then – the signal!

Immediately, I shoot forward, surprising and shocking those around me.

'THE END OF THE WORLD IS UPON US!' I yell. 'According to the Bible, the last days of –'

But the director is not happy. He waves his hands at me, telling me to start again. Immediately, I stop talking and silently return to my staring spot. People look at me, confused, scared.

'Why did he do that?' they are thinking. 'Why did he suddenly shoot forward and start shouting about the Bible and then stop and walk back again? We thought he was harmless!' A mother moves her child to safety.

We go again.

'THE END OF THE WORLD IS UPON US!' I say, but something else is wrong this time, and I get the wave again and walk back.

This is *horrible*. A small gap around me has widened.

'I'm being filmed!' I say, to anyone who'll listen, and pointing desperately into the distance. 'They're up there!'

And even though people look around, they can see no evidence of my secret filmers. I just look paranoid and weird.

We go again.

The Songs

There are three of us in a small, soundproofed booth in a karaoke bar on the outskirts of Chinatown.

We are here for one reason. Marty.

Marty's good. Marty's great. But Marty's *sad*. Because Marty's girlfriend isn't Marty's girlfriend any more.

'Hey,' we'd said, earlier, in the pub, 'stay out. We'll go to a bar, grab some food, see what's happening!'

'I dunno,' he'd said. 'I'm not sure I'm in the mood.'

'Come on,' I'd said. 'It'll take your mind off things!'

And Marty had lifted his eyes, and cracked a short sad smile, and nodded his head, and said, 'Okay.'

And so now here we are – me, Marty and Colin – leafing through a smudged and scruffy ring binder full of badly printed song titles and giggling.

Yeah. *Giggling*. Because Colin and I are getting closer to what we've set out to achieve tonight. We are trying to make Marty think of Something Else.

'Here's what we should do,' says Colin, importantly. 'We each choose a song for the person to the left of us, right? No excuses, no other choices, you find out what it is, you sing your heart out, and that's that!'

'Great!' I say. 'We can do that thing where we belt out the songs and punch the air!'

Marty's eyes light up. I'd only said this because secretly I knew that Marty loves belting out songs and punching the air.

Marty chooses his song for Colin. It's Britney.

Colin stands and belts it out. He punches the air as he does so. He is magnificent. Marty stands and applauds him. This is great! Marty's all better!

Now Colin chooses his song for me. It's Girls Aloud. I take my lead from Colin, doing what I can with the song, making it my own, while making sure I am both belting *and* punching. Now *I* am magnificent, and the look on Marty's face tells me we have now definitely succeeded. We have *definitely* made him think of Something Else. Even if it *is* just Girls Aloud. Colin and I swap a glance and allow ourselves a moment of self-congratulation. What *excellent* friends we are. How *wonderful* of us to be so selfless and giving.

'Well?' says Marty. 'I'm waiting!'

We snap out of it, and both, I imagine, make mental notes to ourselves to remind us to discuss how great we are later.

'Right!' I say, scanning the list of songs. 'Oh! Here's a good one! 4929!'

Colin taps it in, and up it comes: Natalie Imbruglia. 'Torn.'

I smile as the familiar chords start up and start to bob my head in anticipation of the lyrics. 'Marty will have fun with this one,' I think.

And he begins to sing – a beautiful, powerful, tender song about new beginnings, and warmth, and dignity…

I realise we're getting to the part where he'll be able to belt and punch, and I smile to myself. And then I notice Colin's face. He looks absolutely horrified.

Marty has just sung a line about someone showing you what it is to cry.

What? What had Marty just sung? Marty shouldn't be singing about crying! Not now! Not tonight!

Now he's singing about the other person not seeming to know or care what their heart is even used for!

I make a desperate face at Colin. A face I hope tells him that I thought this was a *happy* song! That I'd never really thought about it before! Never studied its lyrics or considered its meaning! It's got that rocky chorus, after all, which is *great* for belting out and punching the air to!

Somehow, I manage to convey all of this by just raising my eyebrows and weakly punching the air. We turn back to Marty. He is lost in his own moment.

He's telling us how he feels. He's closing his eyes and clenching his one free fist and declaring he is all out of faith.

Colin's eyes are wide and mine are wider still. This is *horrible*.

What have I done? What have I done to poor Marty? Poor Marty, who now claims to be naked and cold and lying on the floor!

'Right!' says Colin. 'I hate this song! I'm changing it!'

'Hit random!' I shout. 'Hit random!'

Colin hits the 'Random' button and 'Torn' stops immediately. Marty stares at the screen and says nothing. He looks traumatised. His fists remain clenched and he is breathing a little heavily. Colin throws me an angry glance and shakes his head. There is silence.

We look to the screen.

'Billy Ray Cyrus,' it reads. 'Achy Breaky Heart.'

The music begins.

Marty mouths the words, no sounds able to make it out.

Colin and I stare at the floor.

Lunchiemunchie

Steve sits down for lunch and seems depressed.

'What's wrong?' I say, concerned.

'Nothing,' he says, waving the concern away. 'Let's just order.'

'No,' I say. 'Out with it!'

He stares at me. For the briefest of moments I see a look of despair shoot across his face. A look that says, 'Would that I could, dear friend, but these are woes unique to me, and woes that must remain so.'

Well, it's a look that says a *lot* of that. The rest I just kind of ad-libbed.

We finish our order but Steve is distracted.

'Enjoy your meal,' says the waiter, and Steve says, 'You too.'

I decide to move the conversation on with a joke. Steve is unhappy, after all, and what is better for unhappy people than jokes? I mean being *happy*, yes, but jokes are good too.

'Hey…' I say, beaming. 'What's E.T. short for?'

Steve just looks at me. It becomes clear that there is a time and a place for fun and laughter, and it is not when you are having lunch with me.

'Okay, you want to know?' he says, flinging his arms in the air. 'I'll tell you. It's Jeff in the office.'

I blink once or twice. I hadn't been expecting him to open up so quickly. And I have no idea who Jeff is.

'Jeff?' I say.

'Jeff,' he says, spitting the name out, like a bear might spit out a pizza, if it really had a thing against pizza.

'Who's Jeff?' I say.

'Who's Jeff?' says Steve. 'Jeff. Big-eyes Jeff. Jeff with the eyes. You met him that time. He's got two big eyes.'

'I picked up on that. What's wrong with Big-eyes Jeff?'

At this, he goes all coy.

'It's…a little thing. But little things can build up, you know? It's the office dynamic. The relentless repetition. After a while the smallest thing can grate on you.'

'What's Jeff doing? Is it his two big eyes?'

'It's not his big eyes.'

'So what does he do?'

Steve sighs.

'He says "lunchiemunchie".'

I think about it.

'That doesn't seem so bad, saying "lunchiemunchie",' I say. 'Colin doesn't like it when people say "Londinium".'

'It's not the same as "Londinium"!' he says. 'And he does-n't just *say* "lunchiemunchie". He *screams* "lunchiemunchie". It's more like "LUNCHIEMUNCHIE!"'

I bristle. Steve has just screamed 'LUNCHIEMUNCHIE' in a crowded restaurant. But he's not noticed, so caught up is he in his own little world of anti-lunchiemunchie rage.

'It's every lunchtime,' he froths. 'Without fail. It gets to one o'clock, and it's "LUNCHIEMUNCHIE!"'

'You should stop screaming "lunchiemunchie",' I say, very quietly.

'Exactly! That's what I want to tell him! And it doesn't even have to be lunchtime! Someone just has to *mention* lunch. They could say, "It's lunchtime in Brazil" or "I'm attending a close friend's funeral over lunch", and Jeff'll sit up and yell "lunchie-munchie!" It's got the point where I've started leaving the room when I *suspect* "lunchiemunchie" might be close.'

'You leave the room when you *suspect* it?'

'I leave the room when I suspect it.'

I am filled with concern for my friend. No one needs to be leaving rooms when they merely suspect something might happen. And yet…

'Lunchiemunchie,' I think. '*Lunchiemunchie!*'

'The worst thing is…' Steve sighs, 'it's been seven years.'

He shakes his head, sadly.

'Seven *years*?' I say, shocked. 'For *seven years* this man has been annoying you with his lunchiemunchie? And you've not said a thing?'

He picks at the last of his food.

'Lunchiemunchie,' I think, watching him.

'Have you finished enjoying your meal?' asks the waiter, suddenly there.

'Yes I have,' I say, before realising that sounds rude. 'I mean, I was enjoying it, but now I have finished. Finished *enjoying* it.'

Steve does not look up.

'So what are you going to do?' I ask, as the plates disappear.

Steve looks broken.

'I suppose I *will* have to say something,' he shrugs, putting his credit card on the table.

'Yes,' I say. 'But not yet. Leave it another six or seven years. That's only fair. And by the way, E.T. is short because he has little legs.'

'What?' he says, confused, as if I've not been taking him seriously at all, his eyes widening till they're nearly the same size as Jeff's.

'Thanks for the lunchiemunchie,' I want to say.

I have not told Steve, but just one hour later, I would start to use the word 'lunchiemunchie' on quite a regular basis.

Bauer

I am standing in a branch of a well-known pharmacy on London's Regent Street and I am struggling to decide between two types of bath product. Do I go for the chamomile bath soak with marshmallow, apricot and jojoba extracts? Or do I follow the budget route, and opt for some Lynx Africa shower gel and just pour it in? This is what manhood has come to.

I'm about to plump for the Lynx when I notice a shifty-looking man in filthy clothes hanging around the boxes of incredibly expensive ladies' hair oil products. He does not look like he usually buys incredibly expensive ladies' hair oil products.

And then I realise…he is a thief! Bent on robbing this pharmacy of its goods! I scan the shop, trying to spot a security guard. A couple of bored-looking shop assistants stare, sallow-eyed, into the middle distance. There are cameras, but are they working? Something has to be done!

I've been watching a lot of 24 recently, and in my mind I think I'm Jack Bauer. I hide behind some hairdryers and fiddle about in my pocket until I find some earphones. I pop one in my ear. And then I step out from behind the hairdryers so that the man can see me again. He casts a nervous eye towards me. I look away suddenly, put my finger to my earphone, and pretend to say something into my sleeve. He suddenly leaves the shop.

I have done it! I have stopped a robbery! I am a hero!

I beam, and look around the shop to see if anyone has witnessed my incredible bravery. No. My selfless actions have gone unnoticed. I stand there for a few minutes, thinking maybe I'll be asked to sign a baby or given a medal, then quietly opt for the chamomile bath soak with marshmallow, apricot and jojoba extracts, because I am Jack Bauer, and I need a relaxing bath.

When I get home, I tell my wife of my adventure. She pats my shoulder and tells me I did very well. I decide that she is not patronising me, but that sometimes it must be hard for civilians to fully take in the actions of the few like me. And then nothing happens for a week or two.

But then – incredibly – it is a few weeks later and I am standing in the very same shop, when I look up to notice two shifty-looking men hanging around next to the bathroom technology. One of them picks up a nasal hair remover and pretends to read its box, while the other glances about.

Oh, no. It is happening again. I need to tell someone. I need to find security. I can't try the earphones thing again as I don't have my iPod on me, so I move away from the toothpaste section and towards the door, where I'm hoping there'll be a security guard. There isn't. And then – bang! – one of the men grabs a hairdryer and stuffs it into a bag. The other grabs something else and does the same. They both put their heads down and stride towards the door. I don't know what to do. But I have to do *something*! I am a man! I am *Jack Bauer*! I should body slam him, or twist his arm behind his back and push him through a window.

In the end, I clip his foot with my shoe.

He stumbles and brings his hands out of his pockets to steady himself. He turns back at me and snarls, and I want to say something clever and witty to defuse the situation, but I just calmly say 'Raarrgh', which to this day I don't know the meaning of. And then they leave.

When I get home I write to the pharmacy's head office. 'Dear sir or madam, twice in the past month I have foiled the plans of thieves,in your Regent Street branch. Well, the second time I just tripped him slightly (see CCTV). I feel you may be relying a little too heavily on me in terms of security. It is the duty of each man in this fine country of ours to uphold the law whenever necessary, but I think you should buy a security guard or something. I can offer no guarantees that I will be there when the next thief strikes!'

I felt that hit the right note. Perhaps I'd get a 50p voucher off my next chamomile-based bath soak, or maybe they'd rename their shops after me.

Instead, three days later, I receive the following reply:

> *'Dear Mr Wallace, At no point do we rely on you for our secu-rity, and we would like to strongly disavow you of this notion.'*

I sigh and shake my head. I suppose the sad fact is, society will always be suspicious of those with almost supernaturally heroic tendencies. I now feel I understand Jack Bauer a little better. We are men. Real men. And real men will never be understood by the pencil-pushers. I close my eyes and soak in my chamomile, marshmallow, apricot and jojoba bath, probably just as Jack Bauer was doing right that second too.

Sympathy

It is little over a week since I returned from a Sunday afternoon spent in Leicester at my friend Deepesh's house.

It had been a wonderful day of sitting in the garden in the sun with his mum, dad, granddad, brothers and tiny nephew, the family cat asleep on my lap, the neighbour leaning over the fence, a cup of tea never far away.

We'd all agreed to do it again soon, and then I'd jumped in the car and headed home to London.

But today a text has arrived from Deepesh, and he's not his usual effervescent self.

'Is all okay?' I write, thinking it's probably just in my mind, or that his curt text is just a sign he's busy.

'Not really,' he replies, moments later. 'It's to do with Ned. He's in a pretty bad way.'

I am momentarily confused, until I realise who Ned is. Ned is Deepesh's granddad. I'd always just called him Deepesh's granddad, thinking it a pretty accurate description, overall. But Deepesh's family is a nickname family, and Ned must be short for something.

I write back.

'Is he okay? What's up?'

A few minutes pass by, and I'm strangely nervous, reasoning Deepesh must be trying to work out how to tell me something.

Eventually, a reply arrives.

'Basically, it looks like he hasn't got long. We had him checked out yesterday and they weren't hopeful. Said it could be weeks, not months. We're all pretty sad.'

I don't know how to respond. Poor Deep. But I know that time is of the essence, and I need to quickly let him know I'm there for him.

'Mate,' I write. 'I'm so, so sorry. How is your mum? Is there anything I can do at this end?'

'No,' he replies. 'It's okay. Mum's pretty down, but it's okay.'

'I'm serious,' I instantly write back, wanting him to know he's not alone. 'Do you want to talk?'

'No, it's cool,' he replies, which is understandable.

'Well, anything you need,' I reply. 'If you want me to come back to Leicester, I'll jump straight in the car. If you need to drown your sorrows or anything.'

A few minutes pass.

'It's okay,' he writes.

I nod, put my phone away and walk into the living room, where I tell my wife of Deepesh's troubles.

'Poor guy,' she says, shaking her head.

'Maybe you should text him,' I say. 'He'd appreciate that.'

She agrees and gets her phone out.

'What did you write?' I ask, when she's finished.

'I said, "If you need to get away, please please come and stay with us", and I asked whether I should send his mum some flowers to show we're thinking of her.'

'That's nice,' I think.

Her phone beep-beeps a few minutes later. She picks it up and looks at it.

'Deepesh says, "Thank you, don't worry about the flowers."'

I know he must be upset, but I secretly wish Deepesh would be a little more forthcoming in his appreciation of our good wishes. He must be really upset. Perhaps it's to do with our texting.

'Maybe I should call him later,' I say to my wife. 'Texting seems to somehow cheapen things. It's like a cop out. Maybe it looks like we don't care enough to pick up the phone.'

I shouldn't have just texted back when I'd realised Ned was ill. I should have called. But now that we've established this long line of communications, I can't just call, it'd be overwhelming, so I pick up my phone again and text him once more.

'Deep, let me know when I can call you to talk,' I write, and I pop a little kiss at the end.

Half an hour passes, but I'm certain Deepesh appreciates the sentiment.

Then the reply comes.

'It's sad cos we've had him twelve years but don't worry too much.'

I stare at the message. Twelve years?

The cat. Deep has been talking about the *cat*.

I think back to all the texts. I'd said I was sorry, which was fine. But I'd also offered to drive straight to Leicester. We'd invited him to stay. We'd offered to send his mum flowers. I'd seemed really, *really* upset.

I basically look like I was either being sarcastic or I was having some kind of affair with his cat.

I wonder whether I should come clean, but that would involve me telling him I thought his *granddad* was the one who had weeks to live, and that's not something *anyone* wants to hear.

I'm going to have to just pretend I love his cat.

'Please just keep us updated,' I write, and press Send.

Correspondence

To: Danny Wallace
From: Kieran Mullins
Subject: you

Dear Danny Wallace
I saw you on tv today your a douchebag
kieran

To: Kieran Mullins
From: Danny Wallace
Subject: RE: you

Dear Kieran
   Welcome!! And thank you for subscribing to the Danny Wallace 'Lotsofun' Mailout!!!
   Your first mailout will arrive soon, but remember, you can unsubscribe at any time by simply replying to this email with the word 'Unsubscribe'!

To: Danny Wallace
From: Kieran Mullins

unsubscribe

To: Kieran Mullins
From: Danny Wallace

Dear Kieran

    This week's Danny Wallace Lotsofun Mailout will be out tomorrow! Keep your eyes peeled for plenty of puns and riddles!

    But remember, you can unsubscribe at any time by simply replying to this email with the word 'Unsubscribe'!

To: Danny Wallace
From: Kieran Mullins

Unsubscribe

To: Kieran Mullins
From: Danny Wallace

Dear Kieran,

    It's Danny Wallace here – thank you for subscribing to my weekly Lotsofun Mailout.

    (I've just seen your email. I know what's going on here. Leave it with me.)

To: Danny Wallace
From: Kieran Mullins

what?

To: Internet Abuse and Fraud Department
From: Danny Wallace
Cc: Kieran Mullins
Subject: POTENTIAL INTERNET FRAUD

Dear sirs and madams of the IAFD

Last night I received a message from a member of my Lotsofun fan club, a 'Kieran Mullins'.

It became clear very quickly that Kieran Mullins' email must have been hacked and that whoever has done this has started sending crazy emails to various minor celebrities, calling them all douchebags, etc. It is important that this stops, as it is making Kieran look mental.

I cc Kieran in on this email so you can correspond with him directly.

D Wallace

To: Danny Wallace
From: Kieran Mullins

what are you doing? My email was not hacked, why did you send this

To: Kieran Mullins
From: Danny Wallace

Kieran is going to be really annoyed with you when he finds out what you're doing.

To: Danny Wallace
From: Kieran Mullins

It is me I am kieran

To: Internet Abuse and Fraud Department
From: Danny Wallace
Cc: Kieran Mullins

Sirs and madams,
I forward the latest from the fraudster.

To: Danny Wallace
From: Kieran Mullins

Stop doing this, okay
It is not even a real email address I wrote to them and it
bounced back so stop

To: Danny Wallace
From: Internet Abuse and Fraud Department
Cc: Kieran Mullins

Dear Mr Wallace
   'Mr Mullins' recently sent us an email which we purposely
bounced back to him, using new BounceBack Technology. We
were therefore able to see what email address it came from,
and it does indeed belong to a Kieran Mullins.
   We hope to move straight to prosecution.

To: Danny Wallace
From: Kieran Mullins

Did you set up that email. What is this

To: Danny Wallace
From: Kieran Mullins

Hey

To: Danny Wallace
From: Kieran Mullins

ANSWER me

To: Kieran Mullins
From: Danny Wallace

Hello! Not long now until this week's Danny Wallace Lotsofun Mailout!
**   And remember, you can unsubscribe at any time just by replying with the word APOLOGIES!**

To: Danny Wallace
From: Kieran Mullins

Unsubscribe

To: Kieran Mullins
From: Danny Wallace

UNRECOGNISED WORD

To: Danny Wallace
From: Kieran Mullins

apologies

To: Kieran Mullins
From: Danny Wallace

Accepted!

(no reply)

Conversation Starters for Ladies and Gentlemen: 3

TOPIC 1

I have discovered that those charity muggers who accost you in the street won't stop you and ask you for money if upon approaching them you loudly declare that you are on police business.

I had assumed that this was something to do with a respect for the law, but the weird thing is, it works just as well if you loudly declare you can't stop because you've just murdered someone.

TOPIC 2

I recently received an invitation to a wedding, which it rather pompously informed me would take place in January 2012 AD.

I am pleased that they took the time to be so specific in their planning, but worried also that they trust me so little that they feel the need to make sure I understood the wedding would be taking place in 2012 AD, as if I might get confused and end up attending more than two thousand years before the birth of Christ.

TOPIC 3

If the people who write in to newspapers to complain about the number of repeats on TV really cared about it so much they'd write in when the programmes were first on and not waste so much time.

TOPIC 4

Because it is illegal to talk to a stranger on a train, it can sometimes be confusing when someone stands on your foot or hits you with their briefcase and then fails to say sorry. Which is why I have decided to carry an air horn with me at all times, and when someone stands on my foot I will set it off in their face and then go back to reading my paper. I imagine this will make people want to avoid standing on my feet, but if I've paid good money for the air horn, I'll want to use it, so I'll wear massive clown-shoes while travelling. I'll also wear a red nose and a wig.

Essentially, I really want to get into clowning.

TOPIC 5

If one of your friends or acquaintances ever tells you that they've found Jesus and asks you if you'd like to come to their church, you should definitely say yes, because if they've *really* found Jesus, there's probably a prize or something.

Also, I bet He's got some cracking stories.

And finally

The Man Crush

We are cooking dinner, my wife and I, when she asks me to chop some carrots.

'Oh!' I say, delighted. 'The funniest thing. Dale was saying yesterday that *his* wife makes him chop the carrots at home, and —'

'Oh, *Dale* again, is it?' interrupts my wife, but I think she must have misunderstood, because that definitely wasn't the end of the story. It gets better than that.

'Huh?' I say.

'Don't get me wrong, I'm very much looking forward to this Dale chopping carrots story,' she says, laughing. 'Just as I enjoyed the one about Dale's favourite jeans. But ever since you met Dale, there is very little you say that can't be related back somehow to Dale.'

I am offended. As far as I can remember, I have talked very little of Dale.

'Yes,' says Colin, moodily, waiting for his dinner at the table. 'I've noticed that too.'

To be honest I'd forgotten he was there.

'You're being silly, both of you. I can't remember the last time I mentioned Dale. Anyway…'

'You mentioned him ten minutes ago when you handed me this beer,' says Colin, not looking up. 'You said Dale recommended it, because it's organic.'

'Oh, yeah, well, I did mention him then, yeah,' I say. 'By way of an explanation as to why we've got organic beer and not

Foster's, which if you remember you'd specifically requested as usual.'

'Not everything needs to be organic, Danny,' says Colin, scratching at the label, sniffily. 'Just remember that.'

I turn and look at my wife, confused by Colin's annoyance, and she tries to reassure me by mock-whispering, 'Colin's just a bit jealous of your man crush.'

Ah, well, that explains it. Poor, simple, jealous Colin. He can't know that Dale and I have…

Whoa there.

'My *man crush*?'

'Yeah. You've got a man crush.'

'I haven't got a *man* crush.'

'You've got a *total* man crush on Dale. It's very sweet. Yesterday, how did you describe his hair?'

'I said it was yellow.'

'You said it was *golden*,' says my wife. '*Golden*, like hay in the midday sun.'

'I do not have a man crush on Dale!' I say, defensively. 'I merely admire him. Did I tell you he fixed his own surfboard? He's thinking of applying for *Last Man Standing* if they do another series.'

Colin rolls his eyes and swigs at his beer.

'What?' I say. 'Why are you rolling your eyes? I can't help it if I happen to mention every now and again something about a new friend, like his hobbies, if they're somehow relevant to the conversation, or how the freckles across the bridge of his strong nose remind me of childhood summers in France!'

A pause.

'*What*?' I say.

'I just think this is too much, too soon,' says Colin, looking out the window. 'You met…when? Friday?'

Colin is still upset about this, as *he* was supposed to be with me on Friday, but cancelled, as he'd met a girl he kept saying was 'probiotic' but who actually turned out to be anaemic.

'Yes, Friday. At Pete's house. Dale used to work with Pete in New Zealand, and actually ran his own—'

'Veterinary practice,' says Colin, at exactly the same time as my wife, so I suppose I must have mentioned this before.

I think about it, sadly, as I chop the carrots. Is a man not allowed to be taken with another man? To appreciate his manliness and his vigour? To be impressed by his accomplishments and the neat little scar under his crystal blue eyes that speaks of mystery and intrigue but which was actually caused by a cufflink on a bus?

'You want him to cradle you to sleep,' mutters Colin, interrupting my thoughts.

'What?'

'You want him to cradle you in his big strong arms, because you know that's the only way you'll finally feel safe.'

I look at my wife, puzzled, but she just smiles. I don't know what to say.

So I say, 'Okay, yes, I wouldn't mind. But a man crush is healthy once in a while. And what's more, it'll keep things fresh between you and me, Colin. It'll keep you on your toes! You won't take me for granted any more! Because that can be a real danger in a friendship. Perhaps Dale was sent into our lives to make us realise that. No longer are you to take advantage of our friendship!'

Colin nods, seriously, as if to agree, and then puts his organic beer bottle down.

He gives me those puppy dog eyes.

I give him a fiver, and he pops out to buy some Foster's.

Balloons

I answer the door to my parents and there is something a little odd about the image that greets me.

My dad is grinning broadly while holding a small white balloon on a stick.

'You're holding a little balloon!' I say.

'We stopped for a coffee at a café and they had all these balloons, so we asked if we could take one for our grandson,' he says. 'And here it is!'

Thing is, this is not one of those big silver balloons you might buy from a fat man in a park. It is not in the shape of an animal, nor does it have a celebratory message scrawled across it in giant pink font. It is not a balloon that tells a story or explains itself away. It's just a small white one on a stiff red stick with 'Krispy Kreme' written on it.

'It may have been a mistake,' says my mum, conspiratori-ally. 'No one would sit next to him on the bus.'

I think about how my dad must have looked on the bus, a man in his sixties, grinning to himself and holding a Krispy Kreme balloon. Little wonder he was avoided. He must have looked like a simpleton on a daytrip.

I usher my parents inside, in case the neighbours see these two oddballs, and I wonder whether self-consciousness dis-appears when you become a grandparent.

In the living room, my son adores the balloon.

We rub it on his head and his hair stands on end. It's the first time he's seen such magic.

We play with it for ages, my parents looking on proudly, and I realise it's not just my boy who's learned something today.

How often have I worried what strangers think, when I could have been spellbound instead?

The Magician

There is a trip away planned, and Colin is keen to meet me before I go. We have both been very worried recently that we are becoming predictable in our early middle age. We spend some time deciding where to meet.

'The London Dungeons!' suggests Colin, over the phone. 'We could walk around and learn of ancient torture and mention doubloons.'

'I'm not sure we should go to the London Dungeons. Also, I'm not sure how we'd mention doubloons.'

'We'd just mention them. Just in passing.'

'I don't want to talk about doubloons.'

'The London Eye?'

'Quite pricey.'

Colin thinks about it.

'Keswick Pencil Museum?'

In the end, we meet at a pub just a little further away than the pub we'd normally meet at.

And then…

'Hello, lads.'

A mysterious man with a small moustache is staring at us. He is dressed all in black, with a waistcoat that's just a little ill-fitting, and he is smiling.

'Hello,' we say, exactly in unison.

'Oh,' he says, his hand suddenly on me, on my person, running up and down my lapel. 'Is this…*yours*?'

He grins widely as he pulls his hand away to reveal…

'The six of diamonds!' shrieks Colin. 'The six of diamonds, Dan!'

The man looks proud and Colin looks amazed.

'Well?' says the man, and I don't quite know what to say. I mean, no, it's not mine. It's not often I leave the house after remembering to pick up my keys, my wallet and my phone and then have to return ten minutes later to pick up my six of diamonds. But I want to be a good sport, and so I say, 'Yes! That's my card!'

The man nods and steps closer, and Colin nearly squeals with delight, then says, 'Do another one!'

'All right, fellas? My name's Graydon,' he *nearly* says, because I don't want to tell you his *real* name, because a magician can't reveal his tricks. 'Why don't you pick a card?'

'Me! I'll do it!' says Colin, almost pushing me out of the way, and who has only ever *once* been this excited in a pub before, and that was ten minutes ago when he saw it did Kettle Chips.

'Very well,' says Graydon, fanning out some cards in front of him. 'Any card you like…'

Colin takes his time. He considers one card, then his eyes dart up at Graydon, who pretends to look away, and he quickly grabs another, pulling it close to his chest.

'Now let your friend see,' says Graydon, and as Colin cups it in his hand and bends it towards me, I can't help but notice Graydon does something funny with his other hand. Colin follows my eye and he spots it too.

'Right! Now place your card anywhere in the pack!' says Graydon, and Colin looks at me, sadly. I shrug and nod him on. Colin, deflated, puts the card back in the pack.

'So,' says Graydon, shuffling away and making a great show of things, telling us some kind of story about African Kings and an old poem his auntie used to read him, but we're not really listening now, because we *know* how he does the trick, and it's rubbish, but then suddenly he says: 'Is *this* your card?'

We both stare at him just a second too long.

'Wow!' I say, trying to sound genuine. 'Yes! That is! Colin, tell him!'

'Yesthatismycard,' says Colin, looking at the floor. Though now Graydon seems concerned that Colin is not impressed, so I find myself saying, 'Do another one! Do another one!'

Graydon immediately jumps into action. He 'finds' a new deck in Colin's back pocket, though we both saw him hide it there, then he launches into a new trick, which we both see coming a mile off.

'We can't tip this man,' I whisper to Colin, as Graydon peels off to impress a barmaid. 'He is the worst close-up magician I have ever seen!'

'If we tip him,' says Colin, 'we are only encouraging him. He needs to find himself a girl, settle down. Get a *sensible* job; one he's *good* at.'

We look at each other, and realise we have become quite predictable in our early middle age.

Graydon returns.

'More magic, lads?' he says.

'Yes please, Graydon,' we say, and ten minutes later, to reward him for his dreams, his hope, his *perseverance*, we have given him the biggest tip of his life.

And that, of course, turns out to be his greatest trick of all.

The Invite

It's when I open the envelope that I realise something is wrong.

My wife and I have already been verbally invited to the wedding, and, touched and grateful, we said, *of course!*, *thank you!*, *we'd love to!*

But it's only now, with the silver-lined and heavily embossed invitation in my hand, that I start to understand the *level* of invite we've received.

'Uh-oh,' I say.

'What?' says my wife.

'We're not actually invited to the wedding!' I say, and I make a face that implies this news is almost too grave to deliver.

'How do you mean?' she says.

I hold it up for her to see.

'This invite…is for the *party only!*'

I try and make this sound dramatic, but in reality it just sounds like a cliff-hanger from *The Archers*, so I stress the point even further.

'We are party-only guests!'

This is a disaster. Party only!

Not wedding, not even reception – just the party!

Okay, so we don't know them all that well. But nevertheless, this is terrible news. Not being invited to the wedding-wedding, but only to the after-wedding, essentially means you're on the B-Team of life.

The A-Team? Oh, they get the works. But all you get when you're on the B-Team is a clawing feeling of inadequacy and an uncomfortable disco where the day-drinkers fling off their clothes and talk far too close to your face.

I would argue that only when you realise you're on the B-Team at someone else's wedding do you realise just how they see you as a friend: they *like* you…but they don't like you quite as much as they like their accountant.

I think of how the evening will go and I bristle.

'We'll have to arrive just as everyone else is finishing their meals,' I say. 'And if the reception overruns, we'll have to just stand there and watch them eat tiramisu and slap each other on the backs for being so popular. And they'll all whisper and point at us, as if to say, "Oh, were they not invited to the wedding-wedding? *I* was, definitely. Well, they can't be very good friends at all, can they?"'

My wife looks on the bright side.

'We hardly know them! And maybe it's a tiny wedding. Maybe they can't fit many people into the church. Or maybe it's family only?'

But I know already that it isn't.

'Pete's going to the wedding-wedding,' I say, and I might as well be sticking my bottom lip out. 'Lots of people are going to the wedding-wedding. *We're* only going to the *after*-wedding.'

I toss the invite down on the table, where it spins like a newspaper from a fifties film.

'Well, I will not go, madam!' I say, arrogantly.

'It'll be fun!' says my wife, and after a moment or two I consider her point. Plus, maybe there are some saving graces to being B-level. I start to wonder if by being on the B-Team, we only need to give a B-level present, like a Big Mac Meal or a yo-yo. Perhaps they've made reference to that in the invite.

But no. The gift register makes no allowances for second-tier guest gift-giving. It's still all just stuff made out of pewter. Oh, we've been stitched up, good and proper.

'Maybe we should go off-list,' I say, idly. 'Set our own level. Embrace the anarchy inherent in giving someone a slightly different present from one they were expecting. It'll already cost us to get across the country to that party just so we can stand in a room late at night with some drunk people. Surely going off-list is an acceptable compromise?'

'Come on, we can make a day of it,' says my wife. 'Even though we'll miss all the stuff you love so much.'

'Which stuff?'

'The sermon. The strangers making speeches. The small talk with the cousin of someone you hardly know. The catering.'

Hang about. We'll miss the sermon. The speeches. The small talk and the catering!

Maybe they *do* love us after all!

'Let's get them a really good present!' I say, delighted.

Segue

Sam, who lives down the road, is in a peculiar quandary. There is an American man he has never met but with whom he has been emailing several times a week for some months now. They are business associates, close to making a big deal with one another, but in the past couple of weeks, Sam has not heard a peep from him.

'There was an incident,' says Sam, and he gives me a say-no-more look.

'What kind of incident?' I say, ignoring him.

'An incident over in America,' he says. 'And now I don't know whether I can email him about something as trivial as our deal. I mean, it puts everything in focus, doesn't it, an incident?'

'Yes,' I say. 'But what kind of incident has put everything in focus?'

'It's his brother-in-law,' he says, darkly. 'He's in a coma.'

He says the word 'coma' very quietly, as if by saying it any louder he might attract the attentions of a passing coma himself.

'Blimey,' I say. 'Well, yes, definitely. You should leave him alone. Give him time. I'm sure someone will be in touch when it's right to do so.'

We both sit quietly for a moment and Sam nods to himself, confident he's doing the right thing.

'It's just that it's quite a big deal,' he says. 'I mean, *he* stands to lose out as much as I do.'

'Well, you wouldn't want him losing out,' I say. 'I mean, his brother-in-law is already in a coma.'

'That's what I was thinking,' he says. 'But what do you say in a situation like this? Do I address what's happened, or move past it? How do you segue from coma to deal? I've tried it in my head – it's practically unsegueable.'

'Nothing is unsegueable!' I declare. 'Though I probably wouldn't mention comas. Just use phrases like "You have my sympathy at this difficult time".'

I can tell Sam has mentally filed this away. He taps his chin with his finger, still troubled.

'So how did it happen?' I ask, to fill the silence.

'Well, he nearly drowned,' says Sam, and that's that.

'Swimming?' I say, after a moment.

'No, walking his dogs.'

I decide to leave it there. That's clearly the best thing to do. Leave it there and move on. But something's niggling away at me.

'So was he near a river, or something?'

'Hmm?'

'Was he walking his dogs near a river? Or a pond?'

'No, no, just up in some woods.'

Sam looks away, quickly, clearly implying I should stop asking how this incident occurred, even though it's far too late now. I decide to spell it out for him.

'Sam, how did this man nearly drown walking his dogs in some woods?'

Sam takes a deep breath. He weighs me up, to see if I am worthy of this news, whether I can be trusted.

'It's a terrible story,' he says. 'He tripped and…'

He shakes his head, sadly.

'…he fell in a puddle.'

The words confuse me. I run through the sentence again in my head. It seems a highly unlikely turn of events. It seems… like Sam's associate might be making it up.

'A *puddle?*' I say. 'What do you mean, a puddle? Can people drown in puddles?'

'People drown in puddles every year. And you're not listening to me – he didn't drown. He *nearly* drowned.'

I have to be careful here. I cannot accuse Sam's associate of anything. That would reflect very badly on Sam. But I can't help it.

'How many people drown or nearly drown in puddles?' I say. 'And how do you know so much about it?'

'It happens!' he says. 'I looked it up because I thought maybe it was just a bad excuse.'

'An *excuse?*' I say, pretending that was not the first thing that crossed my mind, too.

'It sounds like one of those so-crazy-it-must-be-true excuses,' he says, pleadingly. 'There's no comeback! I thought maybe he just didn't want to continue with the deal so he said his brother-in-law was in a coma after falling into a puddle.'

'It does seem strange that out of all the excuses in the world, that's the one that topped his shortlist.'

Sam looks petulant. He is a man constrained by ridiculous circumstance. A turn of events that must be treated with all the reverence and respect of a tragedy, no matter how surreal or dubious they seem.

'There *must* be a segue,' I say, determined to save Sam's deal, and now tapping *my* chin. We roll the words around in our mouths for a while.

'Puddle…*deal*…coma…*dogs*…'

Turns out some things *are* unsegueable.

Baby on Board

The day is upon us and I am sick with nerves, for this is a day no man needs to bear.

It has been coming awhile, this day – almost since the calendar began – looming over the darkened mountain in the distance like the rumble of a zombie apocalypse.

But no amount of preparation, no judicious packing nor guidebook tips can save us now.

For we are two adults in an airport. About to board a long-haul flight.

With a baby.

'We are those people,' I whisper to my wife, as I push a tottering pile of bags into the terminal, my eyes scanning the strangers around us, nervously. 'We're *those people*! The ones in airports with bags full of noisy toys and wailing infants strapped to their chests!'

I point at our son who is not wailing at all, but smiling and waving at me, happily.

'We're the people everyone else looks away from, wide-eyed and quick, as if just taking us in for even a second might somehow mean we're definitely on their flight!'

I look her deep in the eye and deliver the killer blow.

'No one here likes us.'

It is true. All sympathy and empathy for new parents goes out of the window on a long-haul flight, which is dangerous, because you shouldn't open windows on long-haul flights.

I had been warned of this day by my friends Nick and Steve, two fellow fathers and members of our monthly Dads' Army meet, during which we drink beers and share war stories and squeeze each other's arms supportively, in case one of us wants to have a little cry.

'You can't do it,' said Nick, gravely. 'If you can avoid it, avoid it.'

'I can't avoid it,' I'd replied.

'Then it is unavoidable,' he'd said, sadly.

Now, in the airport, I look around once more at the people studiously avoiding our eye lest they set off the baby and then have to sit next to him. I am certain this is all anyone is thinking.

'Look how no one is looking at us,' I say. 'They're already angry.'

'It seems unlikely all these people are on our flight,' my wife says, and it's true, because there are thousands of them. I remember Nick's advice from the pub.

'Make use of your sling!' he'd said, wisely, and I'd listened, because he is like a general in our Dads' Army. 'A sling will lull him to sleep. It will also hide him, and hiding him is important, so make sure you hide that baby, because there will be a lot of tutting going on. A lot more tutting than you're used to.'

'That's what I'm afraid of!' I said. 'The tutting! It is the tutting more than anything I fear!'

'You can go to Sling Meets now,' Steve had added, out-of-the-blue, his eyes distant and tired.

'What's a Sling Meet?'

'You go along, and you meet other people who use slings in your region.'

I don't want to say anything, but that sounds rubbish.

'They call it "Baby Wearing". That's what they're all encouraged to call it. That's what I've been told I have to call it.'

'What happens if you don't?'

'I don't know. I might not be allowed to wear the baby.'

Back in the airport, I look at my son again, and I realise something: do I *really* want to hide him? Is that what society has driven us to? Hiding babies on planes? I look around, and I curse David Cameron's Big Society for making me feel bad about wearing a baby. I should celebrate this child, not hide him!

And then it looks like he's about to cry and I step away and look somewhere else, innocently.

'I will wear the baby on the plane,' I tell my wife, coming to terms with our situation. It is intended as a brave and selfless move. I'm taking one for Team Wallace.

'*Wear* the baby?' says my wife, confused.

'That's what people say nowadays. I will strap this child to my chest, and I will walk on that plane, slowly, so that every single person looks into our son's pretty eyes, and sees that he is not like all those other, rubbish babies who cry and moan and whistle. This is a child worthy of their respect! This child is *special*!'

'There's a chance you might come across as a bit special yourself.'

Nevertheless, my decision has been made.

This is the time. The time for me to Man Up. To face down our new enemies. To be a *Dad*.

'*Whistle*?' says my wife.

We board.

As the dawn is upon us, and an orange sun blushes the clouds, stretching through the windows of the plane and reaching around the cabin, I realise: we have *done* it.

It has been a long, long flight, of anxious glances and improvised games, of hurried bounces and surprising toys, of hushed cradling and countless cuddles, but we did it. We achieved our one and only goal.

Our baby did not go crazy and keep four hundred people awake all night.

And now, as the beauty of New Zealand unfolds beneath us, I am heartened and cheered and drunk on relief.

I nudge my wife.

'We were "those people" when we got on this flight,' I say. 'The ones no one wants to look at because they've brought a kid on a plane. But now we are something else. Everybody loves us!'

'He was a good little baby, eh?' says a man, passing us on his way back from the toilet. He leans down and pats our son on the head, and I realise I don't even mind if he's washed his hands or not, so flushed am I with gratitude for his kindness.

This man – and the people all around him – are so relieved to have had uninterrupted sleep that their affection for our son has become artificially heightened. He has, over the course of the last hour, become some kind of in-flight celebrity, like a little fat Stelios, adored and admired by all and sundry. I consider what a pity it is new parents aren't allowed to ask for tips.

'Weren't *you* well behaved?' says a stewardess, leaning in, inches from my son's face, and he smiles, charmingly, as if to say, 'It was a pleasure – and thank *you* for the excellent in-flight service this past day. I will certainly recommend your carrier to my friends.'

We leave the plane on a high, saying goodbye to all our new pals, but soon there is a problem. We have too many bags to fit into one taxi.

'Okay,' I say, taking control. 'You take the baby and a couple of bags. I'll take the buggy and the suitcases in the next cab that comes along.'

I stand alone in the morning sun, waiting for the next cab, considering whether our luck on the return journey will hold. What if our son decides the novelty of very many hours of recycled air in a confined space is not as much fun as it sounds on paper? But that is another day, and I am weirdly happy from the flight still. I wave gregariously as a new cab comes into sight.

'How you going?' says the driver, getting out, and using such a warm voice that instantly and through tiredness I honestly think we could become best friends today.

'Fine!' I say. 'Long flight!'

Then he points at the buggy next to me.

'Where's your baby?' he says.

But I know the man is being funny. He is referring to the fact that the buggy is empty and yet here I am, so I decide to be funny back. I look at the buggy.

'Oh my *GOD!*' I say, staring at it.

I quickly look back so that I can see the delight on his face at this shared joke he started, but there is not delight, there is instead a look of abject horror and confusion.

He's done that slight flinch that people do when they know they have to act quickly but don't know what to do, and his eyebrows are raised and his hands are up.

'No!' I say, suddenly mortified, because I realise he thinks I'm serious. He thinks I left my child on the plane. 'No, I was kidding!'

The man relaxes his shoulders, but still seems tense; angry, even.

'Sorry, I…the baby's in another cab, we had too many bags, and…'

'Got you,' he says, quietly, picking up one of the suitcases and walking it to the back of the car.

I know exactly what he's thinking.

He's thinking, 'What kind of a person jokes about leaving their child on a plane?'

I want to tell him that I don't. I am merely experiencing a heightened sense of well-being and love for the world.

When we arrive after a silent trip to the hotel I discover my wife has booked us in for breakfast.

The baby starts to cry and people glance at us disapprovingly. I'll be honest – my enormous sense of well-being does not last the day.

Irony

I am driving through the middle of almost nowhere, some-where deep inside New Zealand, when I decide to stop for a cup of tea in a very small town indeed.

There are antique shops everywhere, though they do seem to be stretching the definition of 'antique' as far as it will go. I can't help but wonder what would happen if you turned up at the *Antiques Roadshow* with a Jurassic Park mug and a painting of a clown.

I decide this is just the place to buy my wife a lovely present.

I wander into one at random and start to look around. Almost immediately, I spot two fantastic contenders.

One is the strangest doll I have ever seen in my life. It is almost inexplicable, but that does not mean I cannot try and explic it.

It is a doll of a young boy, bent and gurning madly, his fists twisted and clenched in the air, his bottom lip drooping away from a wide-open salmon-pink mouth. A single eye is tight shut – the other terrifyingly wide.

'Dolls to love & cherish' says the packaging, which I think is quite an incredible claim to make of this product, but one which I am only too happy to endorse. I take a surreptitious photo.*

The other contender is a jacket. It is black and white and silky, with enormous puffy sleeves, buttons that look like a

---

* *fig 4, appendix*

beret a mad mouse might wear, lace sewn into the elbows, and...hang on.

'What do you think of this jacket?' says an older lady, sidling up to me.

'Hmm?' I say, surprised.

My phone had been up, ready to take a photo of it. My fellow shopper had obviously seen this, and decided I must be a fan.

'Do you like it?' she says.

She smiles at me, and my instinct is to laugh, but something about this situation tells me I shouldn't. I don't know what to say. What does she want me to say? Does she *want* me to say it's terrible, and then we can laugh about it, and take photos of each other wearing it, and become jacket-friends forever? Or does she want me to say I *like* it, because she designed it, or it used to belong to her, or she was thinking of buying it herself? But that would be madness!

Now she is joined by the lady who owns the shop, and both beam at me, so I shake my head and smile and say, in as non-committal way as possible, 'Look at that, eh?'

This does not seem enough for them. The first lady's smile weakens. They want an opinion! I need to go one way or the other. But which?

'I think it's *terrific*!' I try.

There is a momentary pause, and then the lady breaks into a big smile, and I know I've done the right thing as she takes it off the rail and drapes it across her arms.

'I just like it,' she says. 'I don't know why. It's from 1979.'

She was going to buy it! Thank God I didn't say, 'This is among the worst jackets I have ever seen! It has buttons a mad French mouse would wear as a hat!'

'Were you filming it on your phone?' asks the shopkeeper.

'No!' I say, a little too quickly, but I recover well: 'I was going to take a photo of it. For my wife.'

'Oh,' says the first lady, her face falling slightly. 'Were you going to *buy* it for her?'

'I told you you should've got it yesterday!' says the shopkeeper.

The lady looks at me, sadly, so I make her feel better.

'I will find my wife something else,' I say. 'You should definitely buy it.'

'Are you sure?' she says. 'I do love it.'

'Please,' I say. 'My wife would be angry with me for all sorts of reasons if I bought that and you didn't.'

'What else were you taking photos of?' says the shopkeeper, clearly impressed by my generosity and kindness towards this stranger. 'What else do you like?'

'Oh, you know…' I say. 'Various things. You've got quite a shop here.'

I intend to avoid her line of questioning as much as possible, but she knows she'd seen me take a photo of something else, she's just not quite sure what, but if she finds out it's the hideous doll, she'll know I've been taking ironic photos, and that therefore my opinion on that jacket is…

'Was it the *doll*?' she says, shocked.

'Aw,' says the first lady. 'Let's have a look!'

Jetlag

I am staring at the ceiling at 1.03 a.m. for the second night in a row when I decide to give in. I am home. But I am jetlagged.

I cannot beat this new and powerful enemy just by staring at a ceiling, I decide. So I will get up. Do something useful. Seize the moment! Embrace the day!

I put Modern Warfare 2 into the Xbox and sit down on the sofa.

This is living! I think. This is using the moment! I'd just be asleep now, on any normal day! But not today!

I like to think of playing Modern Warfare 2 as practice, should the aliens ever indeed be living among us and secretly farming our organs. We will need people like me, who can reload weaponry and press buttons. I nod at myself, proud, but I stop short of thanking myself on behalf of humanity. I am modest.

I suddenly feel a little hungry. But it's two in the morning. Doctors say you shouldn't eat at two in the morning, or you'll drown. But it's not two in the morning for *me*. I remember there's a slice of leftover pizza on the kitchen counter downstairs. But it's dark. What if there's also a burglar downstairs? I decide to wait until daybreak. Besides, I'll probably be asleep in a minute.

An hour later, I am listening to 5Live and tidying a drawer. There is a man talking about little fish. I had no idea I knew so little about little fish. I feel like waking my wife and telling her all about little fish. But I'll probably be asleep in a minute, so I wait.

I am still not asleep an hour later. I am watching a documentary on Bravo +1 about the world's most shocking high-speed chases. Some of them are really shocking, but a lot of them are just high-speed chases. I start to really wish I was asleep.

It is five in the morning and starting to get light outside. I creep downstairs and find that slice of pizza. It is a lot smaller than I was expecting. There is wine in the fridge. 'Maybe that will help!' I think. A little wine to get me woozy. Who cares if it's five in the morning? There are no rules on jetlag time! Besides, once I've had it, I'll probably go straight to sleep, and so this still counts as last night's wine, not this morning's wine. I pour myself a beaker of wine, and then, to save myself coming down again later, I take the bottle with me.

Upstairs, I find a game I've never played. Beijing Olympics. I drink wine and practise the skeet shooting. There is nothing wrong with this, I assure myself. There is nothing wrong with boozy skeet shooting at five in the morning.

I start to feel very depressed that I am boozy skeet shooting at five in the morning.

At six, my infant son wakes up. This is great news, though my wife doesn't seem to think so. But we can hang out! I can tell him about little fish and about how I was promoted to Brigadier General on Modern Warfare 2! But they're only up five minutes and then they both go back to sleep. I wander sadly upstairs and watch Charlie Stayt on *BBC Breakfast* interview a man about a thing.

At eight, I have been promoted again on Modern Warfare 2, when I realise: come on! This is not achieving my potential! I've already tidied a drawer in the last seven hours – think what else I could do! I decide to go to the DIY shop and buy some light bulbs, and as I walk there I realise how clever I am being.

I'll stay up today! Get more done! Fight the jetlag! I feel fresh as a daisy and full of the joys of life!

I buy a coffee and maybe six minutes later the wall comes at me fast and furious and things go a bit blurry and a lorry goes by and it's strangely loud and when I get to the DIY shop I forget why I'm there but then I buy a light bulb and a small lock I've got no real use for and I throw the coffee in the bin and trip and stumble home.

'Morning!' says my wife, as I walk through the door. 'Where did you go?'

And I try to say I've been buying locks, but I say I've been lying bocks, and I make it just in time to climb into bed without being sick on my feet.

'Just a nap,' I think, and after ten hours, I'm done.

Later, in bed, I look at the clock.

It's 1.03 a.m. I turn over, and stare at the ceiling.

Mr Parker

Goodness me, what a nice day it's been so far, and what a lot I've got done.

I am energised and full of beans and clap my hands together and think, 'What else can I do today?'

'What else can I do today?' I ask my wife, who is baking a cake.

Let me be clear: my wife does not normally bake cakes, and it is just as rare for me to ask what else I can do. But this is a day of energy and action!

'Well,' she says, 'we were thinking about painting the hallway…'

She must be drunk.

'There's no way I'm painting the hallway,' I say. 'I was thinking more along the lines of fixing a broken pen.'

'I think all our pens are fine now,' she says. 'But the hallway…'

I look at the hallway, sadly. At its grubby and scuffed walls, at the cracks and scratches. Why did I ask what else I could do today?

But then: a brainwave.

'Hey! I'll ask Mr Barker!' I say.

I run upstairs and fire off an email.

'Dear Mr Barker,' it reads. 'We'd like to get our hallway painted. Any chance you could come round and give us a quote?'

A little while later, I get my reply.

'Of course, Danny. Someone will be in touch to arrange a time.'

There. I've done something else today! There is no stopping me! And as I wonder how to celebrate my very many achievements, I stand and walk over to the window, but then hear the *Ping!* of another email.

It's from Mr Barker again.

I click it open.

'Oh, by the way,' it says. 'Maybe Mr Barker can give you the quote…'

I stare at it. This is odd.

'Maybe Mr Barker can give you the quote'?

I shake my head, quietly. Has Mr Barker gone mad? Why is Mr Barker talking about himself in the third person? Is he under the impression that he is a film star, or the Queen? Or has he now taken things further? Does he now insist that even *Mr Barker* must now refer to Mr Barker by the name Mr Barker?

Mr Barker's an oddball, I decide, as I walk out of the room.

But then…

Then I break into a cold sweat. Because Mr Barker is not an oddball. Nor does he think he's the Queen. I run downstairs.

'I think Mr Barker knows I've been writing about him!' I say, as my wife checks on the cake.

'How do you know?'

'Because I asked him for a quote and he said yes and then he sent another one as an afterthought which was all mysterious and said "Maybe Mr Barker can give you the quote…"!'

'Yeah, I think Mr Barker knows.'

'But *how?*'

'Well, Mr Barker is a handyman who's been to our house and you've written about a handyman called Mr Barker who's been to our house.'

I don't know why I did that. Why did I do that?

Usually, I am careful to subtly disguise people's identities. I want no one to feel uncomfortable. I want no one to feel bad. But with Mr Barker it is obvious! Poor Mr Barker! I could have called him Mr Parker! There is no *way* Mr Barker would have cracked that code! He'd probably still have come round, but jealously looked around the place to try and catch a glimpse of his rival, Mr Parker.

'I'm going to have to cancel the quote,' I say, but that is annoying, because then I've sort of done one less thing today.

'You can't cancel Mr Barker,' she says.

'What if I tell him about Mr Parker?' I say. 'What if I say we had a guy called Mr Parker and I changed his name to Mr Barker and it's just an unfortunate coincidence that he does the same job and has had the exact same things happen as Mr Parker?'

'Yes,' says my wife. 'Yes, I think you should definitely do that.'

I do not cancel Mr Barker.

I am expecting him any day, and we've saved him some cake.

The Protest

Today is one of those days.

It is gloriously sunny and wonderfully bright but with frequent and terrifying thundery showers. I look at the evidence, and work out I am clearly at one of the summer's many outdoor music festivals.

Another flu pandemic may only be weeks away, but we are British, and we will gather en masse where we wish.

I am happy. Already, I have eaten a baked potato and made my wife promise me that if ever she catches me wearing a festival hat – something with bells on, maybe, or a wilfully eccentric look-at-me rubber Jester – she will shoot me in one leg.

We stand outside a tent in which a big-name TV comedian is soon to perform, and then it starts raining, so we stand *inside*, but then it *stops* raining, and so we go *outside* again.

As we sit down in front of the giant screen, it begins to gently rain.

'Let's just stay out here,' I say. 'He'll be on in a minute!'

I am looking forward to seeing the big-name TV comedian, because I enjoy his wry eye and I also like his sideways glance at life. It seems I'm not alone, because soon, we're joined by dozens of other people, who clamber past us, and find their own little wet patches of grass to sit on, all eager to enjoy him too. There is a sense of community here in the sunny-and-rainy British countryside, as now hundreds of people sip at their pints and roll their roll-ups and ruffle their children's hair.

I smile at my wife as another festival hat drearily pads past, all callow eyes and lack of imagination, and then I notice a lady trying to find some space in the middle of all the bodies and pints. She finds that space directly in front of me. I shift about and do my best to give her a little extra room, and we smile at each other as she sits heavily on the ground. And then, as is right and proper, she turns her back on me and concentrates on the screen, waiting to see the big-name TV comedian for herself.

'Here he comes!' I whisper, as the compère shouts his name, and on he walks, all likeable self-assurance and cockily casual slacks.

He launches into his act, and the crowd responds with cheers and applause, but I notice that throughout this opening minute, the lady in front of me remains still and stern. That's strange, I think. Perhaps she is deaf, or from foreign shores, because this is *definitely* good stuff. The big-name TV comedian moves into his next routine, and again the crowd responds with nothing but positivity and love…I laugh, and look at my wife, who laughs also, but then I stop. Because once again, the lady in front of me remains entirely still.

'Fair enough,' I shrug. 'Perhaps nothing's hit home yet.' But it is during the big-name TV comedian's next bit, in which he makes fun of a neighbour's budgie, that things take a turn for the worse.

The lady has had enough and harumphs. Making fun of a budgie is clearly against all her opinions on quality entertainment. But rather than simply sit there, stony-faced, she decides to launch a one-woman protest. Silently, and angrily, she turns her back on the screen.

It is quite a statement. I am not sure the big-name TV comedian has noticed, though, because he carries on regardless, and also, he has no way of seeing her.

But *I* have noticed. Because this woman is now approximately eighteen inches from my face, staring straight at me. It is awkward.

'Conform!' I want to shout. 'Stare in the same direction as the rest of us! What kind of maverick *are* you?'

But I do not shout. I merely stop laughing and adopt instead a muted grin, chastened and ashamed that I dared laugh at a budgie. I try and crane my neck to see around her, but that is not good enough, because now she is watching me. Watching my every move.

I don't know what to do. And so I cough very gently, to remind her I am an actual human male, but then I am afraid of starting a flu stampede, and so I stop again, quite quickly.

My wife notices this strange stand-off, how I have been picked as the subject of this woman's ire, and I shrug and make a face which pleads with her not to make a scene. And then she smiles. She reaches into her backpack and pulls out a present for me. A surprise. One she's been saving.

It is an awful festival hat.

Smiling, she places it on my head.

A dreadful moment passes. The woman stares at me. I stare at the woman.

And quietly, she turns back around.

Bullocks

unchtime. Somewhere in central London. A waiter approaches.

'What do you recommend?' asks the woman I'm with: a tall woman, a nice woman, a woman in a lovely suit. We're having a business lunch.

'I'd say you can't really go wrong with the lamb,' smiles the waiter, who must see we are having a business lunch because there is deep understanding and respect in his eyes.

'Then the lamb it is!' she smiles, snapping her menu shut and handing it straight over, like a professional having a professional business lunch. Then it's my turn.

'Can you go wrong with the chicken?' I say, and the waiter does a little half-laugh, and says, 'You can't go wrong with that either.'

I pause, as if I am mercurial and unpredictable, to give the situation some gravitas, because this is a *business* lunch, and then say, 'Yes, I think I'll have the chicken.'

The waiter leaves and I look at the woman, who'd been partway through telling me how much she'd enjoyed watching the Sandra Bullock film *The Blind Side* recently. I'd been secretly hoping she'd forget, so we could talk business.

'What I *love* about what Sandra does,' she'd started, waving a breadstick about, and it was only minutes later that I realised something strange.

'She keeps calling her "Sandra",' I thought to myself. 'Not "Sandra Bullock". If I was telling a story about Sandra

Bullock, I'd call her Sandra Bullock. Everyone calls her Sandra Bullock. Only people who *know* Sandra Bullock call Sandra Bullock Sandra.'

Suddenly, I'm back in the room, as the woman closes her eyes and shakes her head. She's trying to remember something.

'Oh, God, what's it called?' she says, and although I haven't been listening I scrunch up my face to try and imply I'm just as stumped as she is. 'You know – that other Sandra film?'

'She's still doing it!' I think. 'It's not as if she *knows* Sandra Bullock. It's not as if she's *worked* with her. If she'd worked with her, I'd be all for her calling Sandra Bullock Sandra. She could talk about Bobby De Niro and Sam Jackson too, because that's a privilege you earn when you've worked with Bobby and Sam, but don't waltz in here with a breadstick calling Sandra Bullock Sandra when you don't even own a copy of *Miss Congeniality*!'

'Oh – Miss Congeniality?' I try.

'Yes!' she says. '*Thank* you. Anyway…'

'Maybe she's crazy,' I think. 'Maybe she goes home at night and tells Sandra Bullock all about her day. Maybe she's got an email address like "sandyrocks@oddball.com" and owns a cat called Bullocks.'

I watch her as she bangs on about Sandra, oblivious.

'I wonder if she does this with *all* famous people,' I think, blank-eyed. 'I wonder if she says, "Oh, I saw Vernon on the telly last night", or "Trisha's looking tired".'

Actually, it sort of works with Trisha.

And then our food arrives, interrupting her thoughts about Sandra, and I snap out of it and dig in.

But 'Oh dear,' she says. 'Hmm. Oh dear, oh dear…'

'What's wrong?' I say, but she ignores me, and puts her hand up and calls the waiter over. Oh no. I break into a sweat. I can already see what's about to happen.

'Everything okay?' says the waiter.

'Actually, no,' she says, firmly.

'No,' I think. 'No, please, *please* don't do it! We are British! *Please*!'

'I'd like to send the lamb back. I'll take the chicken instead.'

My heart skips a beat. I stare at my chicken, unable to look at the waiter. He picks up her plate and moves away.

She has done it. She has sent her food back.

'This is all Gordon Ramsay's fault,' I think, glowering. 'Showing people how to be all firm and send their food back. Every week in any one of his shows, someone firmly sends their food back. As if anyone ever used to send their food back! Now all people do is send their food back!'

'Over-seasoned,' explains the woman, quietly, conspiratori- ally, and I'm not sure what to do. Where does this new Ramsay attitude, where people talk about how 'honest' their food is, as if a carrot's ever been anything but straight with them, leave the rest of us? What are we supposed to do while the people we're supposed to be having professional business lunches with send their lambs back, all firm and righteous?

I put my fork down next to my rapidly cooling chicken, and realise no one's said anything for a bit.

'Just thinking about Gordon,' I say.

'Who's Gordon?' she asks, confused.

'Sorry,' I say. 'Gordon *Ramsay*.'

'Oh!' she says, delighted. 'Do you *know* him?'

The Plan

Colin seems excited as he takes his seat.

'I've got a new plan,' he says, 'which I intend to try out on my women.'

I frown.

'I'm sorry,' I say. 'You're going to have to run that sentence by me again.'

'My women. The women, Dan.'

I frown again, and shrug.

'Who are your women?'

'The women! The many women I'm intending to see.'

I wave him on. Colin takes a moment, like a grand master revelling in a surprise checkmate.

'So last night I was watching TV, and there was this man. He was a club promoter or something, and he was in a night-club, surrounded by all these girls, and he said he knew Calum Best, and they all swooned. They *swooned*, Dan!'

He sits back in his chair and gives me a what-do-you-think-of-*that*? face.

'So you're going to get to know Calum Best?' I say. 'You're going to somehow finagle your way into Calum Best's social group so you can tell your many women – of whom there are none – that you know him?'

'Don't need to.'

He reaches into his pocket, then slides two phones across the table.

'My phone. And work phone.'

I stare at him blankly.

'So I'm on a date. I leave for a moment. I leave my work phone on the table in front of the girl. I nip round the corner and dial it so it rings right there in front of her. But I've programmed Calum Best's name to come up when my number rings it. She stares at it, sees Calum Best is calling, and when I get back, she's all like, "You just missed a call from Calum Best", and I'm like, "Oh, I'll ring him later" and then she'll go all swoony.'

'Uh-huh. Okay. And what if she *doesn't* say that?'

'Then I'll just stare at my phone and make an annoyed face, like Calum Best just won't stop pestering me, then silently put it away.'

There is so much I want to say. But I settle for 'That is *foolproof*'.

'Doesn't have to be Calum Best, of course,' he says, with a ponderous face. 'No reason why it has to be Calum Best. Could be Quincy Jones.'

'Why would Quincy Jones be calling you?'

He shrugs.

'See how I'm doing?'

'Well,' I say, beaming. 'I cannot wait to see how this plays out.'

Colin beams back and gives me a thumbs up.

'Of course, it's not without risk,' I say.

Now he looks startled. He had at no point contemplated the idea of risk. I continue.

'I mean, what if she picks up?'

'Why would she pick up? Who picks up someone else's phone?'

'She might really want to talk to Calum Best. And then she says, "Hello?" and you're standing in a toilet cubicle and you'll have to pretend to be Calum Best next to all the other men. Do you even know what Calum Best sounds like?'

'I do not.'

'He sounds a little effeminate. Or Quincy Jones? Can you do Quincy Jones without seeming racist?'

'I can't make racist phone calls in a toilet!' says Colin, panicked.

'Who *can* you do an impression of?'

'David Dickinson. And Del Boy.'

It would take a special kind of girl to be impressed by this. The kind of girl literally no one else would touch.

'Okay, let's try it,' says Colin, programming a number into one of his phones. 'You be the girl. I'll leave my work phone here.'

He gets into character and leaves. Moments later, the phone on the table rings.

It says MARTIN SPARKS.

I have no idea who Martin Sparks is. Why would he have written Martin Sparks? Whoever Martin Sparks is, he's not a household name. I go to pick it up and think of something funny to say, but then start to worry this is an actual business call from an actual man named Martin Sparks. I leave it. Moments later Colin reappears.

'Why didn't you pick up?' he says. 'I thought of another impression I could do!'

'I didn't know who Martin Sparks was.'

Colin looks annoyed.

'He was my old geography teacher!'

I consider it.

'This plan to make girls swoon is not as good as it was ten minutes ago, is it?' I say.

Colin quietly puts his phones away.

'Rodney, you *plonker*,' I hear him practising, as we get ready to leave.

The Overnight

I'm on my way to Scotland with my friend Paul when we stop halfway to stay the night at his mother's.

It is not an ideal situation. An ideal situation would be not staying the night at his mother's.

'But don't worry,' says Paul. 'What we'll do is, we'll have a lovely meal, and then we'll head down the pub.'

'That's okay!' I say, because I would not vote for any man who would stop another man from seeing his mother. 'I don't mind! We can just stay in if you like.'

After all, this is only polite. I have known his mother years and years, since I was almost a baby.

'No,' he says, a little too quickly. 'No, we'll go out.'

'I honestly don't mind,' I say.

'No,' he says, again, shaking his head, and looking frightened. '*No.*'

We knock on the door.

'So Danny was saying he fancied the pub tonight,' says Paul, over dinner. He makes a sweeping arm gesture as if he's revealing me for the very first time. He does this just as I'm having trouble biting through some meat. I cover my mouth as his mother looks at me, summing me up as a drunk who can't even bite through meat.

'No, it's okay,' I try and say, food spilling out of my mouth, but she talks over me.

'Is that what *you* want?' she says, and Paul goes all sullen and teenagery.

'So we'll probably head out in a bit,' he says, staring at the table.

'Well, I'll wash your clothes, shall I?' she says, a little frostily, as if that's all Paul ever wants her to do.

I swallow my meat and just smile.

Half an hour later we're at the pub. Paul looks happy. He is free. He becomes very gregarious, and does some impressions, and even wants to go to a club afterwards. But I'm not so sure.

'Do you think your mum would mind?' I say.

His face falls.

'I mean, she's putting us up for the night, and if we're out the whole time...'

'Yeah,' he says, nodding. 'Yeah. I just feel like a child when I'm home.'

'It's nice,' I say. 'It's nice feeling like a child.'

I do not mean this.

We creep into the darkened house. It looks like we've got away with it. She's gone to bed. It is, after all, *imperative* we do *not* appear drunk. But as we get into the hallway we see the kitchen light is on and his mother is still very much up.

'Did you have "*fun*"?' she says, putting the word 'fun' in inverted commas, and putting Paul's pants in the dryer.

'Yes,' says Paul. 'Thunk you.'

We freeze. Paul has said 'thunk you'. Not 'thank you'. '*Thunk* you.' His next sentence better be bloody *brilliant*.

'And now we are home,' he says, carefully, 'safe and sound.'

It is perfect. I'm so proud of him. He leans on the kitchen counter and knocks a spoon onto the floor.

'Well,' I say, covering for him as it clatters about. 'I think I shall head up the wooden hill to Bedfordshire!'

At the time I think this sounds charming but now I look at it written down I have to say it sounds more like the kind of thing a drunk who can't eat meat might say.

Upstairs, I creep about, quietly, trying to get my teeth brushed and myself into bed before his mum comes upstairs. She is a very nice lady but I suppose I can understand how Paul feels. We might be men, but we'll always be boys to her.

Well, *he* will.

I open the door to the spare room and walk in. But I immediately notice there is something wrong here. And then I see what it is. My bag is open. Who's opened my bag?

I rifle through it, and I realise something with horror. My pants and T-shirts are missing.

Paul's mum has washed my pants and T-shirts. I only packed them this morning. They weren't even dirty. And also – I'm in my thirties and she's not my mum.

I feel completely infantilised. She must still think of me as tiny. I want to say something. But I can't. Instead, I close the door and phone my wife.

'Paul's mum has washed my pants!' I say, in disbelief. 'I feel like a child!'

'Well, sometimes it's *nice* to feel like a child,' she says.

She does not mean this.

In the morning, Paul and I put on our pants and drive all the way to Scotland, one of us relieved, the other relieved and just a tiny bit violated.

The Strangers

It is 4 or 5 p.m. and I am standing in an unfamiliar shopping precinct a hundred miles away from home, waiting for my friend to arrive, and a strange thing has just happened.

'Excuse me,' said a giggling girl, with a giggling friend. 'Are you…the BFM Stranger?'

I look at the girl.

'Am I the what?' I say, eyes wide.

'Are you the BFM Stranger?'

'Am I the BFM Stranger?' I say.

'Yes,' she says.

'What's the BFM Stranger?' I ask.

Her eyes widen and she looks at the ground.

'Never mind,' she says, embarrassed. 'Sorry.'

She runs away, giggling, with her giggling friend.

'Well, that was odd,' I think, looking at my watch then scanning the area for my friend.

Five minutes later, I'm approached by a tall and gangly man in a Slipknot T-shirt. He's clearly going to ask me the time, so I start to roll up my sleeve in preparation, but just as I notice he's wearing his own watch, he says, 'Sorry, mate, can I ask you something?'

I nod.

'Are you the BFM Stranger?'

I balk. What's the BFM Stranger? Why do people think I'm the BFM Stranger?

'Um, no, I'm not the BFM Stranger,' I say, apologetically.

'Though you're actually the *second* person to ask me if I'm the BFM Stranger!'

'So you're *not* the BFM Stranger?' he says, ignoring this and continuing to stare at me, like at any moment I might say, 'Oh! The BFM *Stranger*! Sorry, yes, I'm the BFM Stranger, all right!'

I think about how to respond, but settle for a shrug and an 'I'm not.'

This, as far as I'm concerned, has settled the matter.

'*Definitely*?' he says, and for a moment I'm suddenly unsure, and have to really think about it.

'Nope,' I say. 'I can honestly say, I am *not* the BFM Stranger.'

He half-smiles, and nods, and backs away, keeping his eye on me in case it was all my idea of a very clever trick. I pretend to look away and find a pigeon on a bench incredibly fascinating but when I steal a glance back he's still staring at me intently from near a lamppost.

'This must be a joke,' I think, suddenly intimidated. 'Those giggling girls and their intense and lanky friend are having fun at my expense. Maybe a BFM Stranger means something else to the youth of today. I am being *insulted*! Perhaps I am about to get happy slapped! Hang on, do people still happy slap? Could this be a flashmob? Is this 2004?'

I decide to text my friend.

'Hello. No hurry, but do you want to meet somewhere else? I think I am about to get happy slapped.'

His reply is a moment away.

'It's not 2004.'

I make a tsk noise and read on.

'There in a mo. Sorry I'm late.'

I look up, annoyed. I can't leave this precinct now. I have to wait it out. And now – oh, God – someone *else* is staring at me. He's an older man, with his hands in his pockets, and he keeps glancing over at me but pretending he's not. He walks aimlessly up and down, past Ryman's and back, and then, before I know it, he's walking straight towards me at pace and with purpose in his eyes.

''Scuse me,' he says, with bravado.

'Am I the BFM Stranger?' I say, and his face lights up.

'Yes!' he says.

'No,' I say. 'I'm not the BFM Stranger and I don't know why people think I am! I'm just a stranger!'

He looks confused and a little annoyed.

'Just a *stranger*?' he says.

My friend finally arrives with a cheery hello and wants to know what's going on. The older man explains there's been a competition on a local radio station where people are told where 'The Stranger' will be on different days and if they go up and say 'Are you the BFM Stranger?' they win a hundred quid.

'Oh!' I say, laughing. 'I thought it was some kind of insult! I thought I was going to end up somehow *insulted*! Ha ha!'

We all laugh about this.

'But there are other men on their own in this precinct!' I say, cheerily. 'Why would people think *I* was the BFM Stranger?'

The older man thinks about it.

'Maybe it's your stupid hair!' he says, laughing, and my friend joins in.

Maybe we should bring back happy slapping.

Fubble

Colin is looking at me very strangely indeed, because what I've just told him deserves that kind of look. He glances around the café, to make sure no one else is listening, then leans forward.

'You need to keep this very quiet,' he says, quite seriously. 'People will talk.'

'Do you think so?' I say, now worried. 'I'm sure people won't talk.'

'Oh, people will talk, all right. I'll probably talk about it myself later, to some other people, and they'll *definitely* talk.'

'So maybe don't tell them,' I plead. 'You just said to keep this quiet!'

'I said *you* should keep this quiet. *I* can't keep this quiet. I'm going to a party later and I've got no new anecdotes. This is a lifesaver for me.'

What I have just told Colin is that I appear to be the star of very many romantic homoerotic Italian essays.

'So how did this start?' he says, leaning forward. 'How did you end up in so many homoerotic Italian essays?'

I take a deep breath.

'It's that videogame I'm in,' I say, and he nods, as if I've said all I need to say. But then he says 'What about it?' so I guess I haven't.

'Well, the character I play, he's quite bitter and arrogant and sarcastic, and I suppose some people find that quite exciting, especially as he's always making fun of this other character, who's all cool and manly, and…well…'

'What?'

I look him deep in the eye.

'Some people like it when they kiss.'

It's true. And not just kiss. Barely a story goes by without my character – who has my voice and looks like me – walking into a room and ripping someone's shirt off to press his lips against theirs and run his hands through their strong, thick hair, and then say something bitter or sarcastic.

'I even get off with Leonardo da Vinci,' I say, quietly. 'I never thought I'd see the day when I'd get off with Leonardo da Vinci. It just seemed an impossible dream for a boy who grew up in Loughborough.'

Colin taps his chin with his finger.

'I wonder what it is about the idea of you getting off with Leonardo da Vinci that appeals so strongly to the Italian market,' he says. 'And yet Loughborough acts like it never even happened.'

'It *didn't* happen!' I say. 'And it's not me! It's the character! Plus, it's not just the Italian market – there are stories in English, too, and…'

I pause. This is the bit I have been dreading telling Colin. But I must. For the picture is not complete without the final revelation.

'And there's a teenage girl in Germany,' I say, slowly, 'who posts photographs of herself wearing glasses like mine and my clothes and she's had a haircut like me and she's put fake stubble all over her face.'

Colin stares at me, blankly, like this is all too much to take in. I continue.

'She's got a friend who dresses up like the other character and they seem to spend a lot of time snuggling with each other.

Her snuggling as me, and her mate snuggling as the other bloke. There's a whole lot of stubbly snuggling going on.'

There are so many strange levels to my statement that it takes Colin a moment to respond.

'How do you even *make* fake stubble?' he finally says, confused.

'I don't know *how* you make fubble!' I say. 'But she's made fubble!'

'I think the fubble is the tipping point here,' he says. 'The homoerotic stuff is tip-top and adds to your metrosexual credibility, but you need to ask yourself if you are truly comfortable with people spending their afternoons creating fake stubble to then fubble-snuggle. That said, I would appreciate seeing the picture.'

'You're not seeing the picture.'

'I would appreciate seeing the picture of two stubbly teenage German girls snuggling,' he says. 'I'm not being weird.'

I refuse to show him the picture.

'Well, like I say,' he says, blustering on, 'you need to keep this quiet. Don't tweet it, don't write about it, tell no one.'

'But why?' I say.

'I told you: I'm running low on anecdotes, and this one's mine, now. I *own* it.'

I have a think about it.

Basically, that's the only reason I'm telling you all this.

Storytelling

Rich and I have just walked out of the offices of the radio station for which we've spent the morning working.

Everything has gone well. We have played records of our own choosing, to which the public has reacted with gusto and glee. We have interviewed bands, grateful to have been given airtime on one of the nation's coolest stations. We have even managed to time it so that, in the final link, we stopped speaking just at the very second the drums kicked in and the lyrics began...which has made us think we are cool.

The only part of the morning that did not go well was when I'd attempted to tell a story I'd not really worked out very well, about an unfortunate incident that had taken place not twenty-four hours before. I'd been sure it was a good story. But this is something we have subconsciously decided not to talk about. Not today. Not after that last link with the drums went so well.

And so as we leave the station, we wave at the security guards, and they wave back, even though they have no idea who we are, and probably think we were delivering the papers, or perhaps bringing in new sachets of Choc-o-Lot for the Choc-o-Lot machines. This is not enough to bring down our moods.

'Well, *that* went well!' I say to Rich. 'I liked that bit when we played those records, or that bit when we timed it so that in the final link we stopped speaking at just the very moment the drums kicked in!'

Rich smiles at me.

'I liked that bit too!' he says, cheerily. 'And also, I really enjoyed all that Choc-o-Lot.'

I grin, and I nod, and I think about it: I suppose we *are* cool.

Either that, or high on Choco-o-Lot.

'Pint?' says Rich, and we go and have a pint.

Three pints later, we agree we must call it an afternoon.

I trudge towards the tube and buy a cup of tea on the way, and as I get closer to the station, I start to ponder the morning I've had.

'That bit with the drums was good,' I think. 'And also, it was good to have so much Choc-o-Lot. But that *story*...'

I shake my head at the memory of it.

'That story did *not* go well.'

I buy some Wotsits from a man with a quiff and stand on the platform. Beside me, a man chuckles at a quirky story he reads in a freesheet.

'Oh, sure,' I think, sipping my tea. 'Chuckle at a quirky story in a freesheet. But what about my story? I put my heart and *soul* into it...'

A warm wind strokes my cheeks. The train is on its way.

'...and yet,' I think, even though I shouldn't, 'that story did not go well...'

I decide to ignore such bleak thoughts, and shake my head, and bring my tea down, turning as I do so, when...

'Oh! My God! I'm so *sorry*!'

I look at the man. He looks at me. I continue to look at him.

This man. This man who was, moments before, simply holding a freesheet and chuckling, has suddenly undertaken wild and random hand movements and knocked my tea all down the front of me.

I am stunned.

'What were you *doing*?' I say, the train now here. 'Why the wild *hand* movements?'

He looks sheepish. He is well dressed; a bank worker maybe.

'I…' he indicates a CCTV monitor above us. '…I was *waving* at myself on the *telly*!'

He smiles at me as if to say, 'We've *all* done it!' but my entire jacket is soaked, and I'm tired, and, to be honest, I don't think we *have* all knocked tea down strangers while waving at ourselves on CCTV at two in the afternoon. And what's more, as I raise my head after surveying the damage, I notice…he's *legged* it.

I jump on the tube after him.

He is now standing some distance away and I have stepped on board looking like a wild-eyed, tea-obsessed tramp. I stare at him, and he pretends to read his freesheet, even though I *know* he's read the quirkies, and that's what *everyone* saves till the end.

So I decide to stand right next to him, and make him take *responsibility* for his actions, but before I know it's the next stop and he's off the train and down the corridor, and *I* have another *nine stops* with a damp midriff and an empty cup to go.

I stand, wet and stared-at, on my own.

'Still,' I think. 'Good story for tomorrow.'

Next day, on the radio, I tell it.

Afterwards, Rich says nothing, but shakes his head. He cues a song, and stops speaking *just* before the drums kick in and as we sit in silence, I decide I'm going to need a *lot* of Choc-o-Lot today.

Kissy-Kissy

There is a mean kid who seems to live somewhere near the end of our road. I once saw him throwing a cone at a car and now I think that's all he does.

My wife and I are on our way home from having lunch with a bunch of other parents when we see him again. The lunch has been incredibly stressful. My son has somehow learned that when he sees a cup or glass, he should reach out and tip it over. I am struggling to get used to this, because I am not used to having lunch with people who sit down and immediately tip your glass over. It is a rare trait in adults. It doesn't have to be cups or glasses, either. It can be mugs. And at the lunch there were six of them – six little one-year-olds, sharing our narrow table and each one of them trying their best to tip our cups and glasses over. I spent the whole hour moving cups and glasses around, with all the stress of Frogger or Tetris but none of the reward.

'I'm exhausted,' I say to my wife, the pram in front of me. The mean kid is getting closer. He does not seem to have any cones on him, this time, I notice. 'And there's that mean kid.'

My wife smiles. She does not mind the mean kid, who swerves from side to side as he approaches us, as close to a swagger as you can get on a BMX. I suppose he's about nine, and he's always alone, which really does not surprise me one bit.

'I'd love to trip him up one day,' I say to my wife, and she laughs, because it's not like me to want to trip up a child. 'I bet he does bad things to spiders. He's like a bully from the *Beano*.

I bet he creeps about at night, stealing hot pies mothers have left to cool on windowsills. He's probably got a horrible dog that goes into the butcher's and then runs out with a whole string of sausages trailing behind him.'

'You should definitely trip him up,' she says. 'It would make a brilliant court case. You could say that you think he's probably bad to spiders – that could be your closing statement.'

And as we look back, I feel a little guilty about what I've said about the mean kid. But I am utterly gobsmacked at what he then does.

'Did you see that?' I say, in disbelief, as he whizzes by.

My wife is laughing to herself.

'I did see that,' she says.

The mean kid was swerving and swaggering, but right when we looked at him, he narrowed his eyes, and he nodded slowly at my wife, and he puckered his lips, and *he made the kissy-kissy face.*

'He made the kissy-kissy face!' I say. 'At you! My wife! Right in front of me! Your husband!'

It had been a confident and bold play. It was almost admirable in its forthrightness. I shake my head at the sheer meanness of this mean kid. I feel like this nine-year-old boy thinks he can steal my wife.

'He was trying to be all sexy like someone in a rap video,' I say, looking behind me to make sure he wasn't circling us for another go. 'I could never have done that when I was nine! I was still reading the *Beano* when I was nine, and laughing at dogs running out of butchers' with sausages! I wasn't prowling the streets making kissy-kissy faces at civilians' wives!'

I consider trying to gain my wife's sympathies by saying that if the mean kid was a few years older, I would feel completely emasculated by his actions. But then I work it out and that would mean I could be completely emasculated by a twelve-year-old, and that's not something you should really say to girls.

'Are kids getting worse?' I wonder, as we push the pram up our street. 'Or are we just getting old?'

'One way to stay young,' says my wife, 'would be to wait in the bushes and then trip him up.'

Sometimes, I think my wife *wants* me to go to jail.

'When do boys become men, though?' I say. 'Bouncing cones off cars and flirting with women? Does it happen soon?'

I look at my son, sadly.

'Maybe he'll just want to read the *Beano*,' she says, reading my mind. 'Like you.'

Inside, we make some tea and play with our son on the carpet.

He pulls a newspaper off the coffee table and tips my mug over.

But I don't mind.

Noise

I'm sitting in an incredibly loud bar with a posh man who's very drunk.

He's telling me a story – the same story he seems to have been telling me for some time now – which seems to involve the Algarve, a friend of his named Jeremy, and a girl whose name is either Juliet, Julia, or Julius.

'She used to work in a circus!' he says, as the music in the background dips for a moment. 'But don't tell her I told you that!'

I laugh, and shake my head, and promise I definitely won't.

I watch him as he talks. He is having tremendous fun telling me this story. He is having the absolute time of his life. He's hugely animated for one thing, slapping his leg at key moments, and pointing frantically around him at others. And I'm doing my best to be an encouraging listener, and to show him that I too am having the time of my life.

I'm nodding. And saying 'No!' at the unbelievable bits. And shaking my head, and laughing, and nodding some more.

The problem is, I have absolutely no idea what he's talking about.

It's too loud, and he's too drunk, and he's been almost completely inaudible for the vast majority of what seems to be the winning entry in the world's longest story competition.

I've been here ages. And he shows no sign of stopping. He's been drinking here all day, it seems, waiting to meet a friend of his who he says I *have* to meet, and I've been unable to get away, and pretending I can hear his story out of sheer politeness.

He throws his hands up in the air, suddenly, and looks at me, with disbelief all over his face. He's stopped talking, and I have approximately one second to work out how I should react.

'No way!' I say, and he smiles, and slaps me on the leg, and leans in, and I can hear him say 'I *promise* you!'

'When will his mate be here?' I think. 'When can I get out of this without making him feel bad?'

I try and go for my phone, to see what time it is, but he leans in closer, sensing I might not be paying the story my full attention, and wanting me to understand that this moment – this moment he's about to describe – is absolutely *crucial* to the story.

I abandon my phone and look at him intently.

He's close enough for me to hear now, and he says… 'And *that's* when I said enough was enough.'

He leans back in his chair, allowing me to digest that fact.

'Well, good for you!' I say, loudly, one thumb up. 'Quite right.'

He leans back in.

'But do you know what they said in reply?'

I don't even know who 'they' are. I shake my head and stick my bottom lip out. He carries on, very close to my face now.

'They said I was quite right!'

He threw his hands up in the air and said 'Ha!' as if to say, 'this crazy world!', and I made a face which showed I definitely agreed with him on this one.

There was a momentary pause. The man leaned back in his chair and glanced at the door. Maybe this was it. Maybe this was my chance. Perhaps I could get away now – the story was definitely finished. And then, over my shoulder, he spots something…

'Talk of the devil! He's here at last!'

He stands up to greet his friend – who I realise must be Jeremy from the story. And then I realise that doesn't really matter, because I have no idea what the story was.

'J, this is Danny, I'm afraid I've been boring him with stories of our youth!'

'Ha!' says Jeremy, who seems to be just as drunk. 'Don't believe any of it!'

'Ha ha!' I say, and then, because I've got nothing else, 'ha ha.'

'Let me get you a drink,' says the first man. 'Sit down with Danny.'

Jeremy and I sit down, and the man goes off to get some drinks.

And then, just as I'm about to explain that I'd better be going, the man is back over my shoulder, and leans in to say… 'Danny, tell Jeremy what I was saying about the Algarve…'

He looks at me, expectantly.

'Well,' I think to myself. 'Where to begin?'

The Quote

My wife has decided we need a new cupboard in the bathroom.

'Should we buy one?' I say. 'Or get a carpenter in? He could knock something up for a couple of hundred quid and it'll probably end up cheaper if he does it in MDF.'

'Good idea!' says my wife, because it *was* a good idea, and I'm pleased with myself for knowing something about MDF.

Later that afternoon, I'm in town when I get an email from her.

'The carpenter I found says he needs a sketch of what we're after,' it reads, and there, next to it, I see the sketch she must have sent him.

Wow.

It is the worst sketch of a cupboard I have ever seen. I'm not saying I've seen lots of sketches of cupboards, but I really can't imagine there are many that are worse. There are people who've never seen cupboards and have no hands or pens or ink who've probably drawn better cupboards by just scraping their head across a field. This sketch seems to just be some random lines, with random dots, scrawled with a Sharpie by a simpleton. I love my wife, but this time she's gone too far. I wonder what to reply to her, and idly, I scroll up, and good God: there's another one. I think you'll forgive me for being beside myself with shock when I see that this one is even *worse*, because with *this* one she's tried to incorporate a sense of perspective. This was misguided at best.*

I shake my head, wondering if I should talk to her, whether everything's okay with her, and I shrug to myself, because I guess if this is what the carpenter wanted, this is what the carpenter wanted.

An hour later, I'm thinking about heading home, when I get another email on my phone. It's from my wife. I read it. And I read it again.

'The carpenter has given us quite a "surprising" quote for an MDF cupboard, painted eggshell white,' it says. '£2,150, plus VAT, plus parking.'

I blink. And then I have another look at the drawing my wife did. Somehow, this carpenter has taken a look at this psychotic collection of lines and squiggles and thought, 'Yeah. That's about two and a half grand, I reckon.'

Two and a half grand! Immediately, I am bursting with indignation and fury. Who is this man who looks at a child's drawing and thinks he can charge thousands of pounds for it? That sketch looked like an elephant did it. He is attempting to rip us off, I decide!

I find his email and I fire off a reply.

'Dear sir,' I begin, making a pompous face and jabbing at the phone with my most righteous finger. 'I thank you for your quote of £2,150 for an MDF cupboard painted eggshell white based on my wife's drawing. £2,150 seems very reasonable for a small bathroom cupboard painted white. We are concerned that you will not make a profit on this transaction.'

'Ha!' I think. 'Take that!'

'Are you aware that we want *two* little MDF doors, not just one? And both would be painted eggshell white.'

---

* *fig 5, appendix*

Eggshell white indeed! The cheapest of all paints! You could paint all of Luton eggshell white for less than £2,150 plus VAT plus parking.

'It might very well be that my wife's drawing looked too expensive or fancy; perhaps you could provide a similar drawing of your £2,000-vision of our small MDF cupboard.'

'Ha!' I think again. 'Sarcastic and justified! He will rue the day!'

'Perhaps you could provide a revised quote. Remember, though: we want MDF. Many thanks, Danny.'

I am about to press Send, when an afterthought hits me.

'PS. What would it cost in ivory?'

Send!

I feel terrific as I make my way home. I imagine this carpenter in his golden limousine, bank notes fluttering from his pockets as he turns to pick up his phone, which is just a diamond with some buttons on it, and thinking, 'Rumbled at last! For years I have charged thousands to customers based on their terrible drawings. Today I shall retire, and give all my profits to a local children's charity, plus VAT, plus parking. And all because of this one, brave soul, name of Danny.'

I have won! I am a man!

I head for home.

The door of my house flings open, wildly, and I step into the hallway, the conquering hero returned.

I toss my keys onto the shelf with one hand, while dextrously unbuttoning my jacket with the other. I kick my shoes off and they bounce against the wall and bow before me, full of respect and admiration for my magnificent behaviour this afternoon in bringing an errant tradesman down a peg or two.

I stride into the kitchen, in this – my home, my castle – and I see my wife standing by the kettle, shaking her head, looking at her phone.

'I can't believe you sent this email!' she says. 'It's so sarcastic!'

'Yes!' I say. 'But it needed to be done!'

'This isn't like you!' she says.

'Exactly!' I say. 'I feel alive for the first time in years! Did you like the bit where I said I was worried that he wouldn't be able to make a profit by only charging two and a half grand for a small bathroom cupboard painted white? Or the bit where I reminded him we wanted this cupboard made from the very finest MDF?'

'Yeah, but Dan…'

'And all of it based on your sketches!'

'That's the thing.'

'What's the thing?'

'I didn't send those sketches in the end. I took a photo of the space and I just described what we wanted instead.'

My blood starts to run cold. She carries on.

'I mean, his quote is still hugely ridiculous, but…'

'But it wasn't based on your drawings!'

It begins to dawn on me that I have just sent a long and sarcastic email to a probably burly stranger, chastising him for a professional opinion and quote based not on the drawings of a two-year-old, but instead on realistic evidence my wife has wisely forwarded to him.

What do I know about building cupboards? For all I know, they *all* cost two and a half grand.

'Why didn't I just say, "thank you for the quote" and ignore it?' I say. 'Why did I feel the need to respond?'

But I know why. Because I felt it was a slight upon my manhood. Because I felt he had looked at these simple drawings and thought, 'Here is a person with no idea what a cupboard costs. For him, it will cost many thousands of pounds.' Perhaps there is a self-confidence issue at play here. Yes, it is clichéd beyond belief to claim a lack of skill when it comes to DIY, but maybe therein lies a further problem: a paranoia of emasculation and a need to make up for it somehow, anyhow, by showing who the boss is!

And all that would be fine and understandable and maybe even justified. But my email to this man has suddenly gone from knowing, don't-try-that-on-me-sir, to belligerent and sarcastic rudeness!

'God, I wish you could draw properly!' I say, to my wife. 'Then we wouldn't be in this situation!'

I now dread the man's response. With every extra minute he takes to get back to me, he is winning a moral victory. He is making me sweat.

'Maybe he'll never reply,' I think. But that would be worse – because I'd never be able to explain myself.

So I decide to man up, and apologise, for is that not the mark of a true man? No, I may not be good with rawl plugs, nor an electric driller be. But I can write to him again. I can stand up. I can assume responsibility. I can take the blame!

'This is actually all my wife's fault,' I type. 'Please find attached the sketches I thought she'd sent you, for which you were charging £2,150 plus VAT plus parking.'

And in the morning I get a reply.

'Ha ha!' it says.

The Change

The tide has turned and we are not sure whether life will ever be the same again.

'When did this happen?' I ask my wife, standing bleary-eyed in the early morning sun, but I might as well be huddled in the corner, shivering, and she might as well start rocking back and forth, with her arms wrapped tight around her knees, her eyes lost and empty, so shocking have these events been.

'It all seemed to start just this morning,' she says, visibly shaken. 'And look…'

She points at something on the table.

It is a smashed iPhone, cracked and battered and broken. It is clear what has happened here. It has happened before with grapes, with Cheerios, with remote controls and with books. But never before with phones.

And then we hear it again.

The wail. The soul-shattering, nerve-jangling wail.

It is the densest, tensest sound of all, and one that can be triggered by the slightest thing. Perhaps a spoon is not to his liking, or maybe he wants us to watch while he turns the page of a book. We are required to be not just ultra-attentive, but psychic also, and that one's a lot harder.

We rush over. He wants to tap a door but there's a chair in the way.

Christ! *Quickly*! We must respond *quickly*!

We shove the chair to one side and he taps the door then turns round and scuttles off towards the remote controls. We scuttle after him to see if there is anything we can do – anything at all – to help him achieve his new and important goal.

Because that's what our lives have become. Making sure a series of tiny self-set goals can be achieved by our son. And we are living on a knife edge.

'He can't reach that remote!' I cry. 'He can't reach it!'

'Got it!' says my wife and she hands it to him. We stare at him to see if this minuscule delay in satisfaction might yet set him off. But it seems like this time, we're going to get away with it. He fixates on the remote for a second then throws it to the ground and turns round to go back to the door.

We are suddenly placaters, butlers, concierges, porters. We are maids and chefs and hand servants.

'Is this okay?' we say, and we might as well be bowing. 'Is this suitable for you, sir?'

We are two serfs, our nerves permanently shot, perma-smiles fixed awkwardly to our faces in the hope of not angering our tiny god and bringing his wrath down upon us.

How did this happen? It's not like we fed him after midnight.

I'll tell you how it happened: because our baby is no longer just a baby. Our baby is now a *toddler*.

And we are absolutely terrified of him.

No one really admits to being scared of their baby. In the past I have affectionately joked about my son being a fat little aristocrat, metaphorically clicking his fingers and being served the finest foods imaginable while I subsist on Super Noodles and the crusts of pieces of toast he deigns beneath him. When he has finished eating, you can often see me, scrabbling about for scraps, like a dog by some bins, and feeling lucky if there's a bit of pitta bread you can still wipe the drool from.

But that fat little aristocrat is as nothing when compared to the angry Baron that now sits before us, judging us with his serious little face, but then being distracted by a fly and wandering off, pointing.

It is like my wife and I are in a film where the Chuckle Brothers have to look after an insane relative, possibly played by John Candy, who makes crazy demands and stamps his little feet or suddenly collapses to the ground in floods of tears because he's not allowed to turn the gas knob on the oven or steer the car.

My wife and I pad around the house in total fear, avoiding every known creak in the floorboards, disabling the doorbell so the grumpy Baron can have his rest, or embarking on a series of the most arduous journeys imaginable, such as round and round the sofa fifteen or twenty times at 6.14 a.m.

Having a baby is tiring enough. It's like someone's come into your house and hidden a series of alarm clocks that you know could go off at any time and make it impossible to relax. But a toddler is like someone's thrown an Ewok through your window and he's found his way to the Red Bull in your fridge.

I talk things through with my friend Nick, while my wife arranges a replacement phone, which luckily is a better model.

'It all comes from love,' says Nick. 'He loves you and trusts you implicitly and just doesn't understand yet why he's not allowed to wipe eye make-up on your lamps. He wants to share the experiences. It all comes from love.'

And then I understand. And the fear subsides. And the long walks around the sofa become *our* walks, not just his. He smiles at me, and I'm full of adoration for this perfect little toddler.

When my wife's not watching, I hand him my phone.

If he really loves me, he'll get *me* an upgrade, too.

Aimless

The phone rings just as Friday night is beginning and I answer it.

'Hello?'

'Danny? It's Steve!'

It's Steve.

'How's it going?' he says. 'What you up to?'

The truth is, I am not up to much. The baby has had his bath and gone to bed. A curry is on its way and a movie is downloading as we speak.

'Not much!' I say. 'Just about to relax for the evening.'

'Aaah,' says Steve. 'I love it when it's that time to relax for the evening.'

There's a pause.

'Yes, that's a good time,' I say, and there's another pause. 'So what can I do for you?'

'No, nothing really. Just thought I'd phone up for a bit of a chat.'

Oh, no. One of Steve's aimless chats. The problem with an aimless chat is precisely that there's no aim. No set end. There's nowhere for us to agree to head for a satisfying resolution we can both be happy with. But rebuffing an aimless chat is like rebuffing the very person who's proposed it. It is like laughing in their face, and shouting, 'You are wasting my time, sir! Begone!' which is actually pretty cool, because you don't get to say 'begone' much any more.

'Oh, okay,' I say, glancing at the clock. 'So what's the news?'

'No, no news, really.'

I can hear the baby start to stir through the baby monitor. The phone must've woken him.

'Right,' I say. 'Well, there's not much news here, either.'

An early out! I could be free already! But now the baby's started to cry.

'Is that the baby?' says Steve.

'Yes,' I say, because after all, it's not my wife. But I'm pleased he's heard, because never has there been a better excuse to end an aimless chat. 'I should probably—'

'Wow, he's loud…!'

'Yes…I should probably pop up and—'

'Does he wake up a lot?'

The crying gets louder and I hear my wife dash upstairs. I'm all for friendly chats, but this one must now be over.

'So…what you doing tonight?' says Steve. Apparently it's not.

But then I say: 'Oh!'

'What's up? Doorbell?'

'Yes, it's the man with our curry, so—'

'Oh, I'd *love* a curry,' says Steve.

'I should answer that.'

'What kind did you get?'

The doorbell goes again and the crying upstairs amplifies.

'Um…butter chicken and a beef madras,' I say, moving to the door. 'So anyway…'

'You should save some for breakfast,' he says. 'Cold curry! It's like that with pizza, isn't it?'

'Ha ha, yes,' I say, but I'm not really listening, because I've opened the door and I'm fishing in my pocket for change.

'You giving him a tip?' says Steve.

'I am, yes,' I say. 'So listen, let's catch up in the week, and—'

'How's your mum?' he says.

'She's good,' I say. 'I think she's about to ring, actually, so I'd better—'

'Tell her hello from me!' he says, as I awkwardly shut the door and carry the curry through to the kitchen. 'And your dad.'

'Will do! Okay, then, well…'

'How *is* your dad?'

'*Begone!*' I want to shout, but it is vital he does not feel rebuffed!

'Um, Dad's actually got a bit of a cold, so I'd better keep the line—'

'Okay, sure. Hey, get him to stick some Vicks VapoRub in a bowl of hot water then put a towel over his head and breathe in the fumes. That's what I do.'

'I'll mention that, yes. Okay, then, well, our food is ready, so…'

'The fumes will clear his nose, if it's nasal.'

'Okay!'

'*Is* it nasal?'

'I think nasal is an element. Right! Curry time!'

'*Curries* are good for colds. Maybe you should say—'

'Good idea!'

'Right! Well, enjoy it!' he says, and I get ready to put the phone back in its cradle.

'We will! Okay, cheers, Steve…'

My wife walks into the kitchen, the baby calmed and asleep again.

'Yeah, I might get a Chinese or something.'

'Okay, well, bye!'

'Maybe pizza.'

Click.

Friday night can begin!

The curry is average. The movie is bad. Steve texts to tell me he's ordered beef madras too, while my wife assures me sometimes it actually *is* okay to rebuff.

Bottoms

We're crossing the roundabout just near McDonald's, me and my son, and he's sitting in his buggy, happily pointing at big red buses.

We're on our way to Gymboree, where we'll sing and dance and push giant inflatable logs around and he'll be kissed on the head by a sinister stuffed clown named Gymbo. But as we walk in my heart sinks ever so slightly. Because it becomes very apparent very quickly that I am the only dad here.

Being the only dad somewhere is difficult. The pressure is on. You feel like your every move is under an intensified scrutiny. There's no gangly, fumbling colleague to share the burden, there's no one at the same parental pay grade to exchange knowing glances with, there is just you and a room full of strangers you're sure must secretly be judging you.

I pretend this does not bother me and take off my son's little blue duffle coat. By which I mean I take it off *him* – I don't go around wearing my son's little blue duffle coat.

We hold hands as we walk to the tiny indoor slides, and then…I see the first one of the day.

Damn it.

I jerk my head away, instantly, but my goodness – there's another one, over there, just peeping out by the window. That's two already!

I knew this would happen. This is why I don't like being the only dad at Gymboree.

I am surrounded – surrounded! – by inadvertently exposed bottoms.

I wonder what it is about being a young mother that means you no longer care if people see your bottom. Because I have seen more bottoms since becoming a father than all the bottoms I ever saw as a non-father put together. My whole life is just young women's half-exposed bottoms.

(Note to self: this would look terrific *on a T-shirt.)*

Some men are now thinking, 'Well, that doesn't sound so bad, all these young women's bottoms', but those men are mistaken and foolish and one day will rue the day. For these are not *romantic* bottoms. These are not bottoms intent on seduction. Only men pressed up against the windows of stag party mini-vans have perfected mooning as seduction.

No, these bottoms are the *other* kind of bottoms. They're tired, exhausted bottoms. They're pale, hopeless bottoms whose very appearance in society says, 'Look, what do you want? I'm a bottom who's had three hours' sleep. There's probably a Cheerio stuck to me somewhere. Please, for the love of all that is good and holy, leave this bottom alone.'

And that's what I want to do. I want no trouble. I just want to go about my business, unburdened by their sudden aggressive appearance in my life.

I check my belt and hoist my jeans up a little. At least *I'm* fine.

'Let's all form a circle!' says the Gymboree leader, and a couple of jokes pop into my head but I decide to leave them.

We all kneel down next to our children and start to sing a song. But already I am feeling quiet and withdrawn. I hope I am not letting my son down, by being here but not being his mum. I wonder if when she's here with him she gets her bottom out. I hope this is not what he has come to expect from us when in large groups. It will make weddings and christenings uncomfortable.

Beside me, a woman allows her toddler to stagger into the middle of the circle, but she's nervous about him falling, so she leans as far forward as she can, while her jeans stay exactly where they are.

'Oh dear God,' I think, and stare at the ceiling.

After forty-five minutes of this, Gymboree is over, and Gymbo the Clown does his rounds, kissing each baby on the head.

'No wonder he has to paint that smile on his face,' I think. 'Poor Gymbo. The things he's seen.'

When we get home, my wife sits facing me in the living room, drinking coffee with her friend, who has brought round her newborn. I want to tell them about all the bottoms, about the painful suburban traumas of life as a dad, but maybe now is not the right time, and maybe this is the wrong audience, so instead I decide just to grow up.

I smile, pop my hand on my wife's friend's shoulder and stoop down, over her shoulder, to kiss her on the cheek.

As I'm down there, I notice that just inches away she is breastfeeding her child.

I sigh, and traipse upstairs, and decide to just keep out of trouble.

The Speech

I don't know why we didn't do this sooner.

It's late at night in a curry house near a market, and for the past several hours I've been surrounded by old friends from university, brought back together for one night only to reminisce and share good food.

There have been a few surprise appearances, and even a video, put together by Caroline, which must have taken absolutely ages.

Everyone applauds as the video ends, and we all wonder how Caroline managed to find all that old footage and all those old photos, and how long she spent ordering it and editing it and crafting it.

And then the desserts arrive and everyone goes back to eating and chatting.

'Someone should really say something,' I say to my friend Espen, who's come all the way from Norway especially for this. 'You know – thank Caroline for all her hard work on that video and say how nice it is we're all back together for one night.'

'Yes,' he says, solemnly. '*You* should do it.'

'No,' I say. 'Maybe it should come from you. You came all this way.'

'Well, maybe you could thank me, as well.'

'Yes, you should absolutely be thanked,' I say. 'So maybe Amar should do it.'

'This was all Amar's idea, though.'

'I see what you're saying. You're saying *he* should be thanked too.'

Espen nods, importantly. I look around the room. Everyone is just talking. 'But someone should *say* something!' I think. 'We need a focal moment. Something to bring it all together! Something where we can feel all warm and fuzzy and the right people are thanked for all their hard work.'

'Okay, I'll do it,' I say, and I stand up and bang a glass with a knife.

'Excuse me,' I say, and people turn to listen, understanding this is an important moment. 'I just wanted to say how great it is we're all back here together. To old friends!'

Everyone says 'To old friends!' in exactly the way I've just said it and raises their glasses. It's quite satisfying and gives me confidence.

'Yes,' I say. 'And also, we should thank those people who've made it really special.'

I look first at Espen, next to me.

'He came all the way from Norway just to be here tonight – ladies and gentlemen – Espen!'

Everyone cheers and whoops and Espen raises one hand to take the people's gratitude, magnanimously, like some kind of bashful superhero.

'For having the idea and finding the venue and arranging it all – Amar!'

Now everyone cheers and whoops for Amar, and he too raises his hand to wave away their gratitude.

'And finally…' I say, and I turn to the girl whose supreme efforts and dedication, so rare and so wonderful and so inspiring, have really impressed and touched us all…and I completely forget her name.

I smile. I glance across the table. Dozens of eyes are upon me. They are expecting great things. Touching words.

But her name! What's her name!? I just said it to Espen a minute ago! I saw this girl every day for three years! We're Facebook friends! I *know* this!

'…wasn't that a great video, before?' I say, and I start to applaud, and everyone joins in. I'm buying myself time. I glance at Espen for help but he can't help me because he's still coasting on his own applause and couldn't possibly realise what's happened here. Why would he?

'It was a terrific video. And gosh, it must've taken so much work to put together.'

A thought.

'How *did* you put that together?' I ask her, hoping perhaps something she says or the way she says it will jog something in me.

'Just old footage,' she says and she shrugs.

It jogs nothing.

Oh, why did I think that making a speech was a good idea? Because I am too kind, that's why. I am too good a person! Well, never again. Never again will I make a speech to thank anybody for anything. Not if this is the way things go. Not if this is the way I'm thanked for it!

'Well, it was a terrific piece of work,' I say. 'So please – raise your glasses…'

No! What am I saying? I'm not ready!

'And be upstanding…'

Why am I moving to the end? How am I going to do this? I start to panic.

A *C*! It begins with a C! Carol?

'And let's all really say thank you…'

Can I risk it? Can I take that risk?

I look at her.

'…to *this* girl!'

I do a weird bend and point at her with my both my fingers and say 'This girl!' in a funny way, which I hope implies so much familiarity and friendliness that mere 'names' mean nothing to us any more.

'To Caroline!' says everyone in the room, in unison.

'CAROLINE!' I say, straight after, making sure everyone can hear and kicking myself. 'To Caroline.'

'You completely got away with that,' says Espen five minutes later. And then Jan says it. Amar just winks at me. Caroline remains silent on the matter.

Which makes me think that actually, I might not have gotten away with it at all.

First Things Last

There are three of us in this pub in Stoke Newington, staring bleakly at our drinks. We meet here sometimes, now. We meet because we are the only ones who know.

We are members of a secret underworld. A club, of sorts. You witnessed our initiation. And now, when we pass others of our kind – in the street, maybe, or in a park or shop – we nod, silently. It is a nod that says, 'I know you, traveller. I know your world. You may pass in peace this day' – a bit like vampires probably do, or at least members of a classic car club. We are the daywalkers.

We are dads, and we are yet to speak properly about this, you and me.

'Nice, this place,' says Steve, opposite, swirling round the last of the ice in his drink. 'Kid-friendly.'

'Yeah,' says Nick, whose T-shirt bears the stain-within-stains of a thousand hours of drool. 'Kid-friendly. Plus, plenty of corners, if your wife doesn't want to expose a teat.'

This, more than anything, sums up my year.

We didn't used to talk like this. We used to talk of men things. We used to tell tales of honour and valour and bravery. I imagine. I also imagine that very rarely did these tales ever include the word 'teat'.

'Ah yes,' I think, with grim solemnity. 'We would sit in pubs like this, rain battering the window, day turning to night, and we would do it often. It would not be a special occasion. It would not be for a mere hour or two. It just *was*.'

Now we are merely three tired men who've met up for a lunchtime cola on our way to do other dad-based things.

From the outside – for anyone looking through this window – we probably look quite normal. But if you have kids, you know full well that these people are not like you. They don't know.

They have never heard of MacLarens or Bugaboos, and will be unable to tell you the very specific pros and cons of each. They have no need of Mr Tumble. They know not of Timmy Time. They know nothing of BabyBjörns, or ZingZillas, or the Family sections you find in weekend-edition newspapers you now don't have time to read. They live their lives, in fact, without the faintest idea that newspapers even *have* a Family section.

'A *Family* section?' they will say, in their clean clothes, as they meet for drinks after work, because they bloody can. 'Do you mean the Sport section? I think you mean the Sport section because there's definitely one of those. Although I've heard of Rastamouse, if that helps?'

And yet we were once like them.

Now, I'm afraid, we are only like each other. I am dirty like you are, tired like you are, and, since you asked, yes, *we* opted for the Bugaboo too, it was the reversible handle option that really sold it for us, but it's such a minefield, isn't it, plus John Lewis deliver, which is a *godsend*.

'I need to pick up a teething ring,' says dirty, tired Steve, as much to remind himself as anything, his brain bruised by baby-jetlag. Nick loudly announces the closest place, and how much one costs. It's like a snap reaction, the way other men fire pellets of football trivia.

Nick's on his second child. He is a corporal in our makeshift Dads' Army, formed those few months ago in that café. He wears a permanent look of hard, dishevelled chaos. He has the look of a man who has seen things – awful, *terrible* things – that he cannot speak about and hopes we never raise. He also has glitter on his collar and a felt-tip chicken scrawled on his hand.

'I need to be back by two,' he says, staring into the middle distance. He doesn't say why and we, scared, don't ask.

Now, I know what you're thinking. You're thinking, 'Christ. Anyone would think you were the first people to become dads!'

Well, you're being ridiculous, and I hope you realise that.

We are perfectly aware that our dads were dads also. The crucial difference is that they were *always* dads. They were born, then they were dads, and there was nothing in between, just enough to fill a couple of old photographs in which they're wearing too-short shorts or have weird hair. Do you see? *Our* dads are just *dads*. With us, it's different. We *did* things before! We used to stay up late, and go out, and spend Saturdays playing Xbox and ordering curry after curry and texting each other and pushing each other into hedges.

And yet these memories – of wasted Sundays and free evenings and trips to the cinema and not being able to walk past a pub that looks like fun – very quickly become startlingly vague. A blink of an eye ago, my son was just an idea, and yet ask me to remember what life was like before and I struggle. Because, as you know, being a dad, or being a mum, is quite the greatest thing in the world.

There is not one person on this earth who, upon seeing a heavily pregnant woman, does not take great delight in saying, 'Your life's about to *change!*'

'Change how?' you think. 'Change right away? Change for ever or just for a bit? Will I ever play Xbox again? When will I next push someone into a hedge?'

And then come the firsts…the first things you read about in this book.

Like when I saw him for the first time – bent down and kissed him for the first time. When he slept on my chest for the first time, gripped my finger with the whole of his tiny hand for the first time. When I drove him home for the first time – slowly, through London traffic, praying other drivers took extra care this special day, understanding those bright yellow Baby on Board signs for the very first time. And when I carried him indoors, and showed him his home – full of love, love just for him – for the very first time.

Inside, that day, we drew the curtains and dimmed the lights. We spoke lightly and with care. We created our cocoon and sat with him, on the sofa, just staring at him. That's something no one ever mentions when they tell you how your life will change. They mean you won't sleep as much and you might have to change cars. But no one ever tells you how much staring you'll do. Quiet, soulful staring. You study every flicker, every moment, every breath, every twitch of a finger or sigh. Evenings melt away into nothing. Half-watched box sets spill their DVDs, untouched since the night before this all happened, never to be finished, destined only to grow dustier.

And at some point – maybe earlier than this, maybe right at this moment – the terrifying weight of responsibility makes itself known.

'He can't do *anything*!' I remember telling Colin, who probably thought I was talking about him. 'He needs us to do *everything*. Otherwise he'll just…lie there.'

I'm not sure what I'd been expecting him to do. It's not like I thought he was going to make us a sandwich, or pop to the shops. And I'm not saying I thought he was lazy – though babies are *notoriously* immature.

I'm just saying that at some point you finish thinking, 'this is mine' and you realise: '*we* are *his*'. His *everything*.

I had phoned my friend Julian for advice. He has twin toddler boys. He is like a *colonel* in the Dads' Army.

'You'll be okay,' he'd said. 'You're only having one. You can get away with only having one. We've got two. It's like the siege of Sarajevo at our house.'

Another friend put it like this: 'Remember in *Apocalypse Now*? When I got my son home, I felt like the Martin Sheen character. He's running around in the trenches during a battle, and he finds a soldier, and he asks him who's in charge. And the soldier looks at him, and says, "Ain't *you*?"'

It can be no coincidence that these Dads' Army recruits use war metaphors to explain fatherhood.

From that point on, the firsts just keep on coming. Then there's the first adventure outdoors, nervously swerving your pram down a side street if there's even a hint of a rumour of a dog nearby. The first smile. The first unusual rash you spot, the first anxious googling of the symptoms, the first time you realise that with 3.8 billion search results returned it's probably something quite common.

There are the first sleepless nights, of course, and it would be remiss of me to pretend they don't happen. There are the first ear-piercing, nerve-jangling, out-of-nowhere screams. The first signs of teething…the first signs of a tooth.

Which reminds me…

'We could walk through the park and go and get your teething ring,' I say to Steve. It is a sentence that, had you asked me last year, I'd never have expected to say.

'I need to be back by two,' says Nick, having presumably forgotten he said it about five minutes ago. Again, we don't ask him why.

Together, we walk, three men bonded by fatherhood, a small Dads' Army platoon on an important support mission for supplies.

We are all without prams or slings, of course, so to the Normals, we appear to be just mates on a road. A pram, we have found, is like an invisibility cloak. People just don't see you any more. A sling lets you sidle through society without detection too, ignored by everyone and unnoticed everywhere except for the queue to get on a long-distance flight.

'Did I tell you about the sling meets you can attend?' says Steve, but if you remember, he has, and several times.

It's quite nice, this. Life is quieter, somehow.

We pass another pub, and see some guys about our age, enjoying an early pint. One of them's just said something funny, and his friend pushes his arm in a shut-up kind of way. Another man stands to get a round. Everyone laughs again.

We have all seen this glimpse of a different time.

But none of us wants to stop, not even for a second.

End

Appendix

figure 1 – *Pizza terribile con Pepe Arancione*

figure 2a – Vegetarian Sandwich, not Mike's Way

figure 2b – Vegetarian Sandwich, not Mike's Way either

figure 3 – Big in Egypt

figure 4 – Dolls to love & cherish

figure 5 – £2,500 RRP

figure 1 – Pizza terribile con Pepe Arancione

figure 2a – Vegetarian Sandwich, not Mike's Way

figure 2b – Vegetarian Sandwich, not Mike's Way either

figure 3 – Big in Egypt

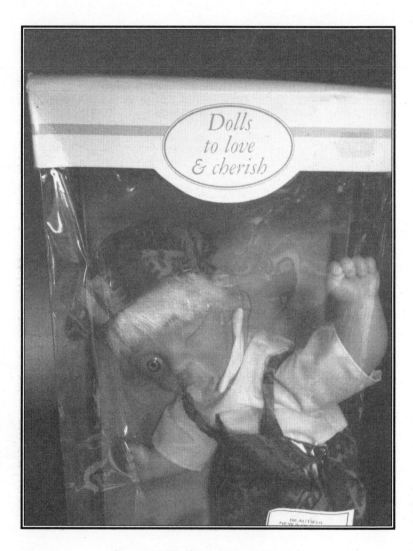

figure 4 – Dolls to love & cherish

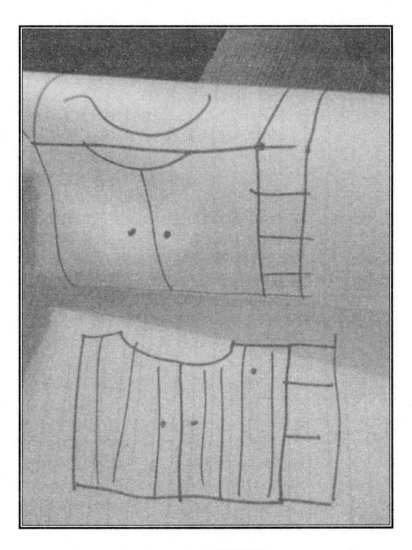

figure 5 – £2,500 RRP

Danny would like to thank...

Greta & Elliot Wallace. Ian & Trudy Wallace. William Sansom.

The brilliant *ShortList* gang – Phil, Terri, Howard, Jamie, the whole dang lot of you.

Jake Lingwood, Simon Trewin, Lisa Thomas, Ed Griffiths, Katie Johnson.

Tiffany Daniel, David Heyman, Peter Roth.

Tony Hale, Laura Prepon.

Howard Sanders, Lauren Meltzner, Jago Irwin, Jeff & Jackie Filgo, Mike Murphy, Andy Ackerman, Ric Swartzlander, Erin Wehrenberg, Wendy Steinhoff, Suzanne Patmore-Gibbs, Samie Falvey, Lynn Barber, Steve McPherson.

Rebecca Glenn. Steve Chamberlain. The very generous and lovely Meral Ali. Richard & Rebecca Bacon, Marc Haynes, Richard Glover, Wag Marshall-Page, Jake Yapp, Julian Barratt, Marty Umanski, Xavier McMahon, Anil Tailor, Mr Barker, and everyone else who makes an appearance in this book, whether by real name or not.

And, of course, you.

Thanks.

www.dannywallace.com